P9-CFN-637

the human machine

« AN OWNER'S GUIDE TO THE BODY »

MAIN LIBRARY
Champaign Public Library
200 West Green Street
Champaign, Illinois 61820-5193

RICHARD WALKER

CONTENTS

OXFORD
UNIVERSITY PRESS

Oxford University Press is a department of the University of Oxford. It furthers the University's objective of excellence in research, scholarship, and education by publishing worldwide in

Oxford New York

Auckland Cape Town Dar es Salaam Hong Kong Karachi Kuala Lumpur Madrid Melbourne Mexico City Nairobi New Delhi Shanghai Taipei Toronto

With offices in

Argentina Austria Brazil Chile Czech Republic France Greece Guatemala Hungary Italy Japan Poland Portugal Singapore South Korea Switzerland Thailand Turkey Ukraine Vietnam

Oxford is a registered trade mark of Oxford University Press Inc.

Text © Oxford University Press 2008

The moral rights of the author have been asserted

Database right Oxford University Press (maker)

First published 2008

All rights reserved. No part of this publication may be reproduced, stored in a retrieval system, or transmitted, in any form or by any means, without the prior permission in writing of Oxford University Press.

Library of Congress Cataloging-in-Publication Data is available.

ISBN: 9780192728647

10 9 8 7 6 5 4 3 2 1

Originated by Oxford University Press
Created by Harris & Wilson

Printed in Thailand

6 WELCOME PAGE

7 HOW TO USE THIS BOOK

8-9 SYSTEM CHECK

10-11 KEY FEATURES

12-13 PRODUCT SPECIFICATION

14-15 PRODUCT LIFE SPAN

16-17 COMPONENT CHECKLIST

18-19 EXTERNAL FEATURES

20-21 LOOK INSIDE

22-23 MACHINE INSTRUCTIONS

24-25 BIOMECHANICS

26-27 WIRING AND COMMUNICATION

28-29 INTERNAL TRANSPORT

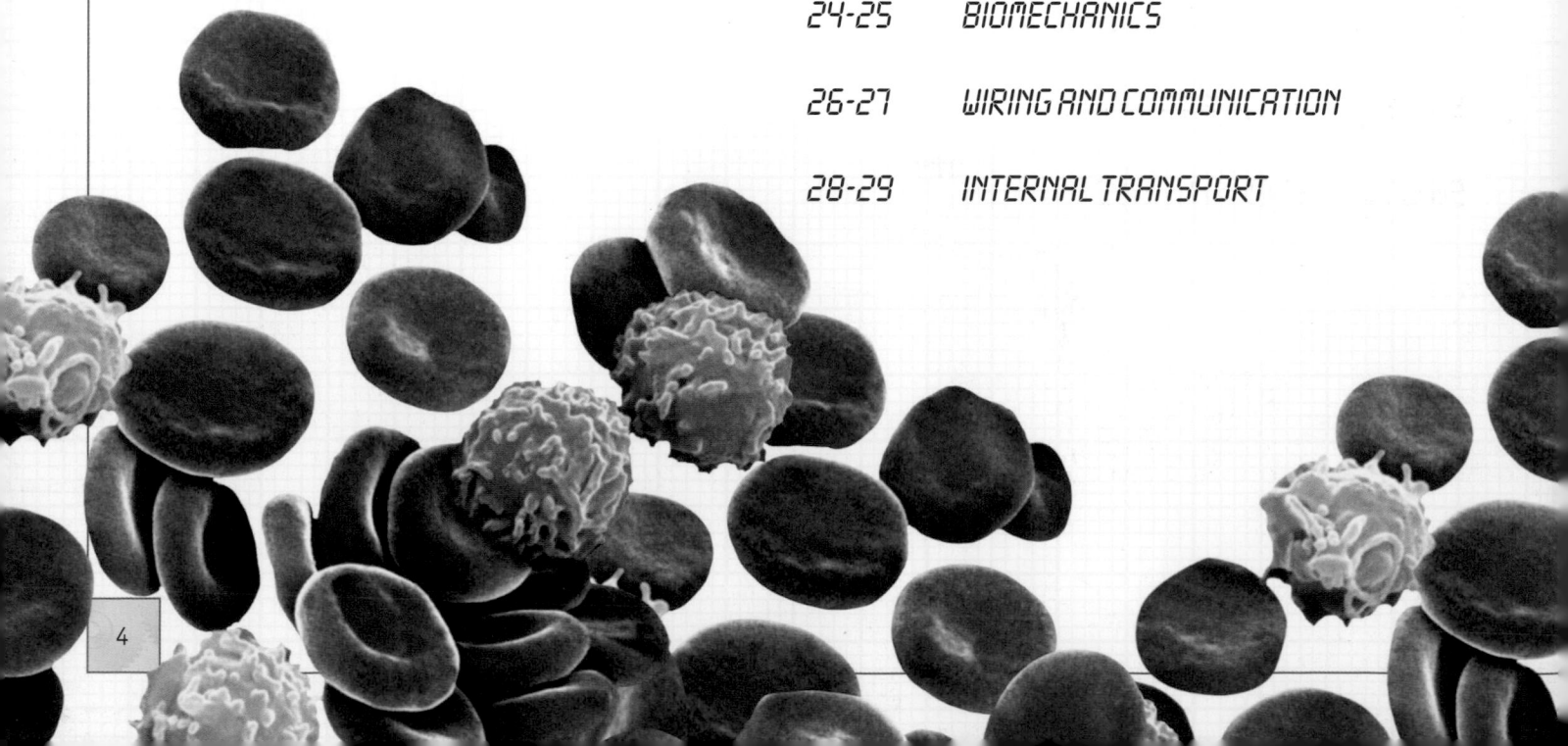

30-31 AUTOMATIC OPERATIONS
32-33 VENTILATION
34-35 REFUELING
36-37 ONBOARD COMPUTER
38-39 PREPROGRAMMED FEATURES
40-41 SHUTDOWN MODE
42-43 ENVIRONMENTAL SENSORS
44-45 VISUAL DISPLAY UNIT
46-47 OPTICAL TESTS
48-49 COMMUNICATION SYSTEMS
50-51 HEATING AND COOLING
52-53 CHEMICAL CONTROL
54-55 WASTE AND WATER
56-57 SURVIVAL MODE
58-59 MAINTENANCE AND UPGRADES
60-61 BUILT-IN PROTECTION
62-63 EMERGENCY MODE
64-65 TECHNICAL SUPPORT
66-67 TROUBLESHOOTING TIPS
68-69 MECHANICAL FAILURE
70-71 PARTS AND UPGRADES
72-73 WEBLINKS
74-77 GLOSSARY
78-79 INDEX
80 ACKNOWLEDGMENTS

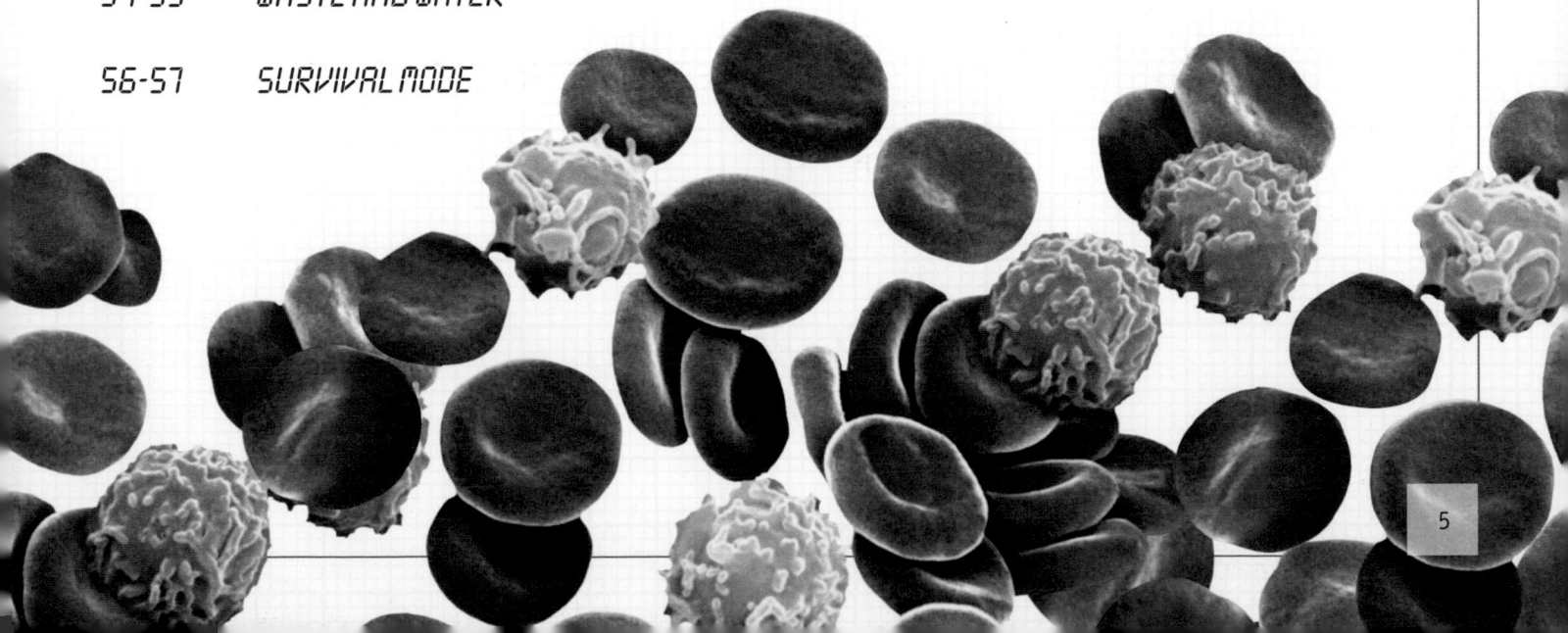

WELCOME PAGE

We share our planet with an incredible range of life—millions of species of animals, plants, fungi, and microorganisms. Although we are the most intelligent of all life-forms, we are, like other creatures, biological machines that walk, feed, drink, and behave. And, in our case, talk, create, think, and remember.

The Human Machine is a unique guide to the human body and the way it works. It is a user's manual that covers every aspect of body activities, including troubleshooting and repairs. On each and every page of this book you can discover everything you need to know and understand about the body's huge range of operations.

Like any manual, *The Human Machine* is highly organized. Check out any aspect of the body machine's workings and you will be presented with the categories you can see opposite. What better way, as an owner, to discover more about your body and how it works.

Richard Walker

Richard Walker PhD

HOW TO USE THIS BOOK

RIVAL PRODUCTS
Take a look beyond the human species to see how animal and plants perform and compare with us.

? TRUE OR FALSE?
Tricky, testing statements will make you question whether they are real facts or mere inventions.

DESIGN FEATURES
At a glance, this enables you to pick out the key features of every aspect of the human machine.

ADDITIONAL DATA
Here's an extra snippet of information that adds to the main theme and gives you more insight into the body's workings.

SPOT CHECK
A chance to test your knowledge with multiple choice questions. The answers are found at the foot of the right-hand page.

TOP TIP
See how to make the most of your life in terms of health, diet, exercise, and general well-being.

WEBLINK KEYWORD
Turn to pages 72–73 for a full, indexed list of websites that will add to your understanding of the human machine.

SYSTEM CHECK

Teamwork makes the human machine operate efficiently. The "team" consists of twelve specialized body systems that interact and work together to produce a walking, talking human being. Let's check on some of those systems.

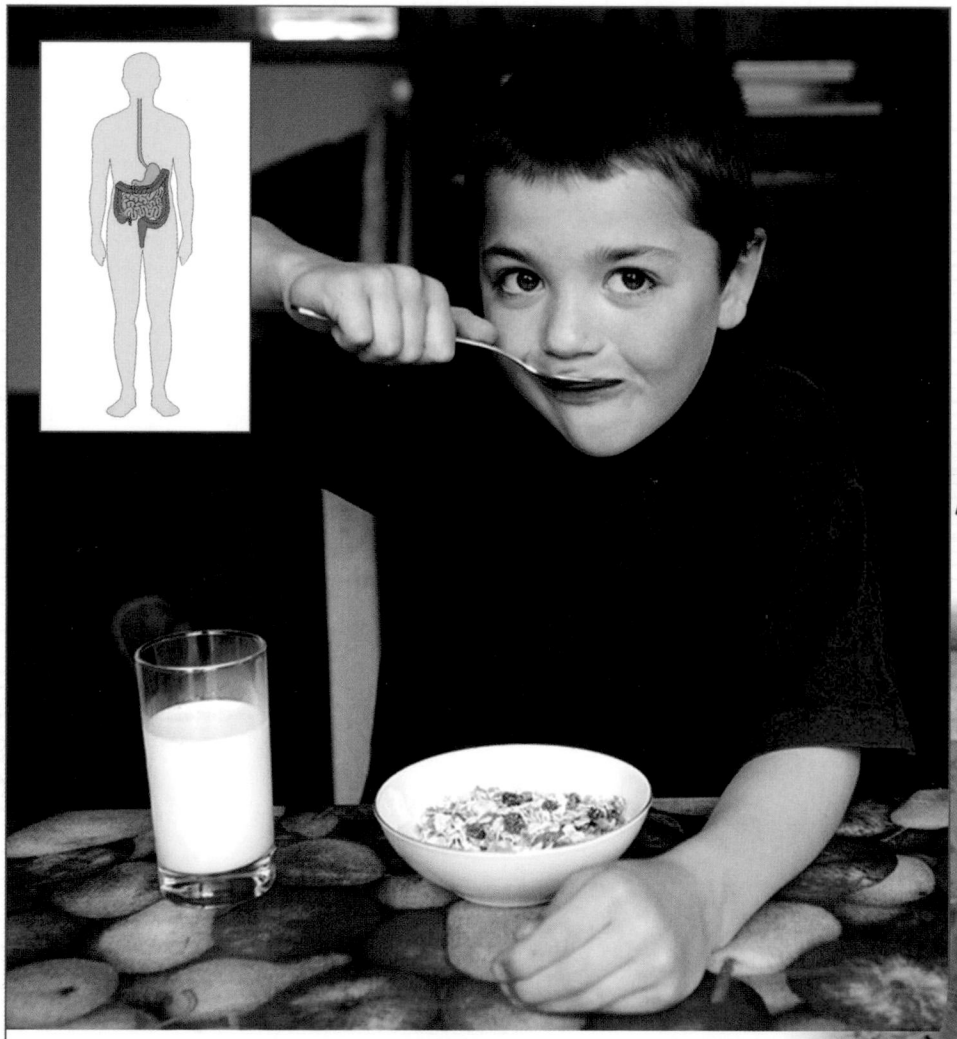

FUELING

Your mouth is the entrance to the digestive system. This long, tubular system gets food into the body, then breaks it down into very simple substances. The body uses these to provide the energy it needs to work, along with the raw materials required to repair it and make it grow.

CONTROL

You can see and understand the words and pictures in this book because of your nervous system. It also enables you to feel the pages, smell lunch, remember what happened yesterday, invent stories, and throw a ball without falling over. In fact, the nervous system controls just about everything we do. And like other body machine systems it is made up of component parts called organs—in this case, the brain, spinal cord, and nerves.

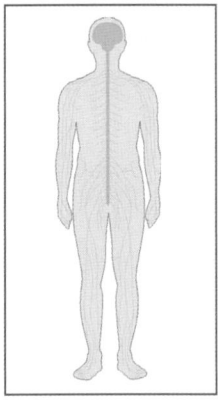

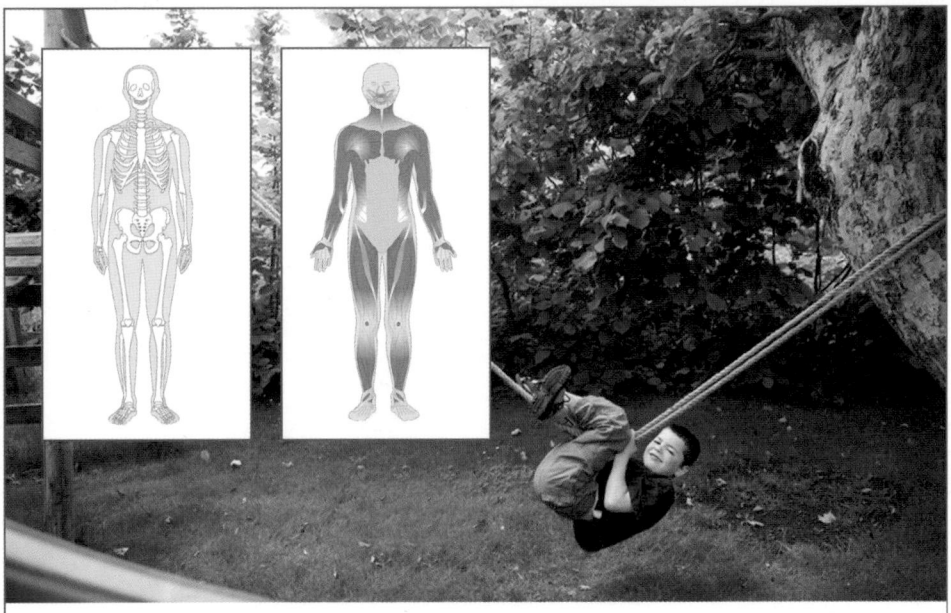

MOVEMENT

Two systems keep you upright, give the human machine its shape, and allow you to move. These are the skeletal and muscular systems. The skeleton is a flexible scaffolding made of bones, which is pulled by muscles so you can perform a vast array of movements from writing to climbing a rope.

DELIVERY

Without vital supplies, the body machine wouldn't last long. The breathing system gets oxygen into the body. The circulatory (blood) system carries oxygen, food, and other essentials to every single part of the body.

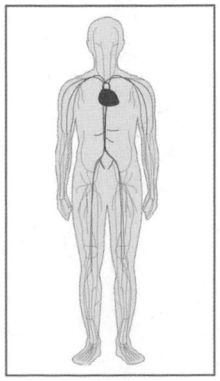

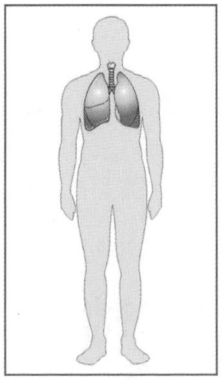

KEY FEATURES

Each of us has our own individual appearance and personality, but we also share key features. Our bodies, built from trillions of cells using the same master plan, grow and age in identical ways.

PRODUCT SPECIFICATION

Every body machine is constructed to the same pattern with minor variations in certain features, such as height, weight, shape, eye color, and personality. These differences distinguish us one from another and make each of us unique. But otherwise we are all the same—brainy animals with upright bodies supported by two legs, and with hands free to reach out and grasp.

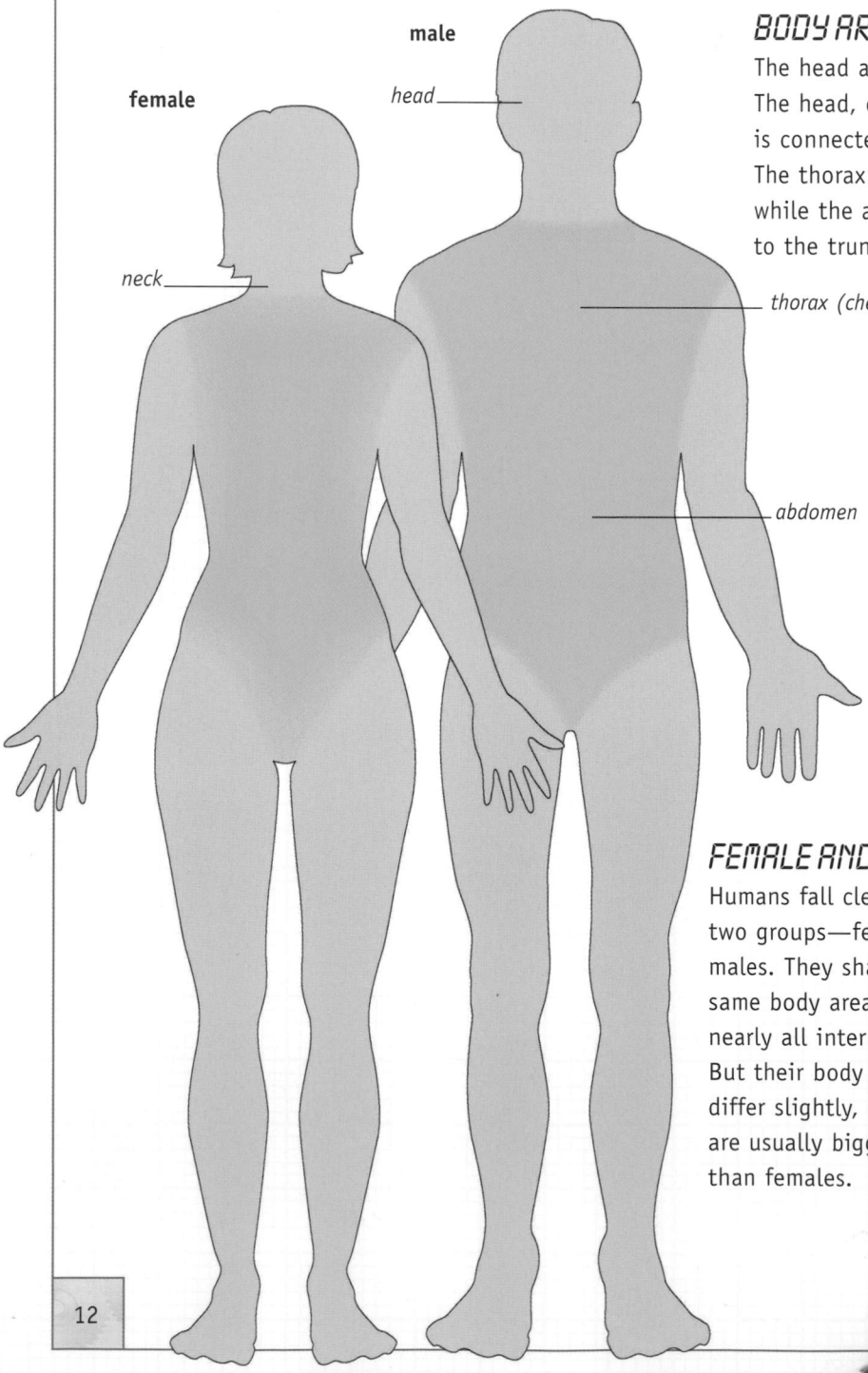

BODY AREAS

The head and trunk form the body's main axis. The head, containing the brain and sense organs, is connected to the trunk (blue) by the neck. The thorax (chest) is the upper part of the trunk, while the abdomen forms its lower part. Attached to the trunk are the limbs, the legs, and the arms.

HUMAN VARIETY

Around the world, people show wide variation in hair type and color, facial shape, skin color, and other external features. But these differences are minor and reflect how, in the past, we adapted to local climate conditions. In terms of our genes, all humans are very closely related.

FEMALE AND MALE

Humans fall clearly into two groups—females and males. They share the same body areas and nearly all internal organs. But their body shapes differ slightly, and men are usually bigger than females.

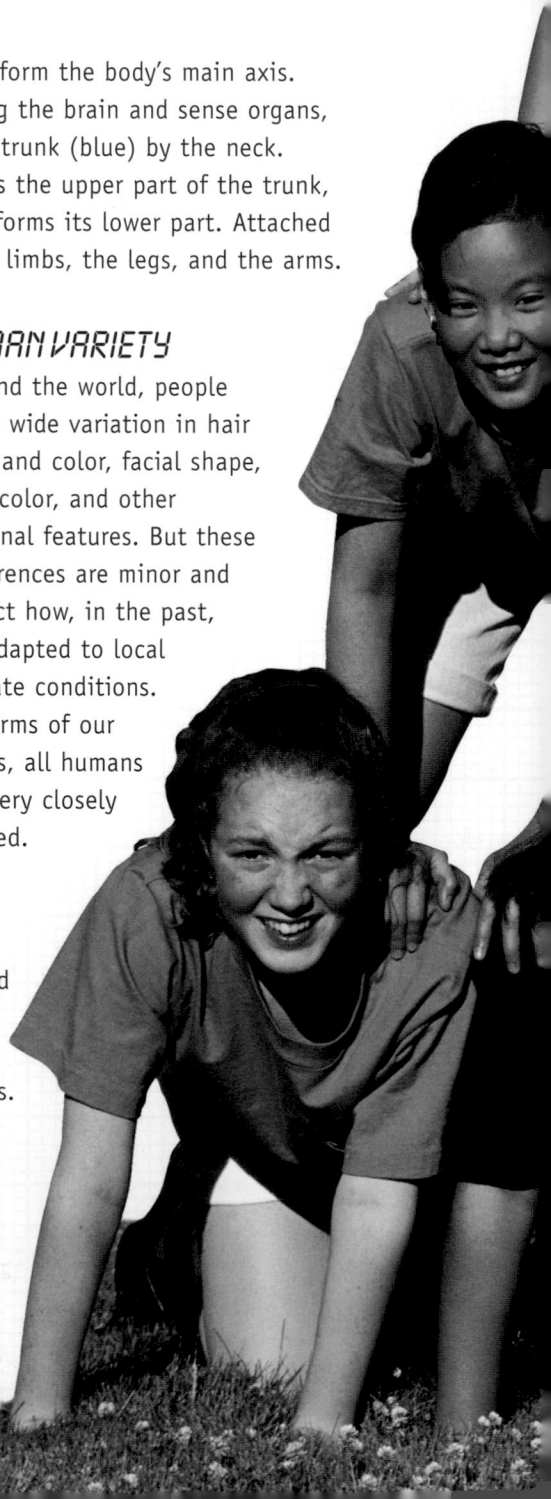

? TRUE OR FALSE?

We have just as many hairs as chimpanzees —just shorter

DESIGN FEATURES

- Ability to walk on two legs
- Hands free to perform tasks
- Opposable thumb enables hand to grip objects and make tools
- Short body hair means humans can sweat to keep cool
- Flexible arms and shoulders
- Large brain size means greater intelligence.

RIVAL PRODUCTS

Humans belong to a group of animals called mammals. These are animals with fur that feed their young on milk. Today, while we big-brained humans thrive, other mammals, including gorillas, pandas, and tigers, are threatened with extinction.

SPOT CHECK

Q. How many humans are there on Earth?

a) Around 6 billion
b) Around 60 million
c) Around 6 million.

WEB LINK KEYWORD **SPECIFICATION**

Answers: True or False? – True; Spot Check – a)

PRODUCT LIFE SPAN

Every living thing on Earth has an expected life span—the period of weeks, months, or years it is expected to remain alive. But how long can the human machine be expected to keep on working and how can we make it run for longer? Crucial factors include genes (inherited instructions) and the machine's lifestyle.

RECORD BREAKERS

Wherever we look in the animal and plant worlds there are examples of individuals living to the extremes of their normal life span. At 122, Frenchwoman Jeanne Calment (1875–1997) has the longest confirmed human life span. That's nothing compared with Adwaita, a giant tortoise that died aged 250 in 2006. But this Californian bristlecone pine was already 300 years old when the Egyptian pyramids were being built 4,700 years ago.

RIVAL PRODUCTS

For most animals, the bigger they are, the longer they live. But that's not the only factor. If it was, humans would have the same life span as pigs (10 years). Another key factor is the ratio between brain and body sizes. With big brains and smallish bodies we live far longer than predicted by body size alone.

Mouse *3 years* | **Rabbit** *9 years* | **Dog** *12 years* | **Penguin** *15 years* | **Kangaroo** *18 years* | **Gorilla** *35 years*

? TRUE OR FALSE?

One day humans may be able to live to 150

LIFE PROFILE

During its life, the body machine goes through a set sequence of physical changes. During childhood, the body grows rapidly. Adolescence involves a growth spurt, and the child changes into an adult. In adulthood, growth is completed. In later life, the skin wrinkles, hair grays, and the machine becomes less efficient until it stops working altogether.

DESIGN FEATURES

- Parental care for offspring can continue to 18 years
- Brain designed for rapid learning in first 15 years
- Built-in replacement schedule.

TOP TIP

TO LIVE TO 100:

Avoid too much sun

Avoid stress

Eat well

Get regular exercise

Macaw *50 years* | **Dolphin** *65 years* | **Elephant** *75 years* | **Human** *80 years*

ADDITIONAL DATA

Birds have life spans that are much longer than would be predicted by their body or brain sizes. So, if you want to live longer, sprout wings, and learn to fly!

SPOT CHECK

Q. Which country has the longest life expectancy?

a) USA b) Russia c) Japan.

WEB LINK KEYWORD **LIFE SPAN**

Answers: Spot Check – c), then a), then b); True or false? – Maybe

COMPONENT CHECKLIST

The basic components of the body machine are microscopic living structures called cells. There are over 200 different types of cells in the body. Cells of the same type are organized into communities called tissues while different types of tissues work together to form organs, such as the heart and brain. This organization converts a shapeless mound of cells into a living human being.

CELL STRUCTURE

Cells may be small but they're not simple. Each is a self-contained living unit with an outer membrane, a controlling nucleus, and, between the two, a jellylike cytoplasm. Within the cytoplasm are various tiny organelles, each with their own task. Mitochondria supply energy to make things work, while ER and the Golgi body make, store, and transport materials.

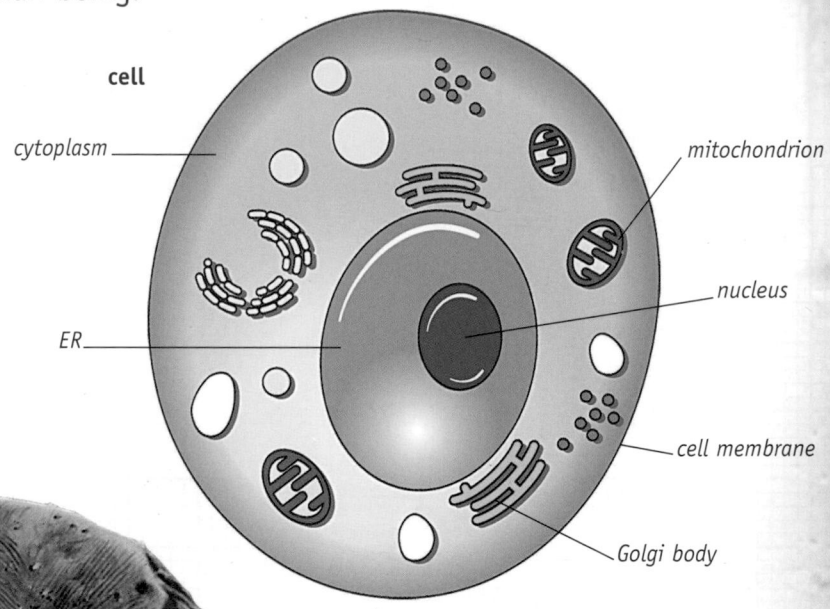

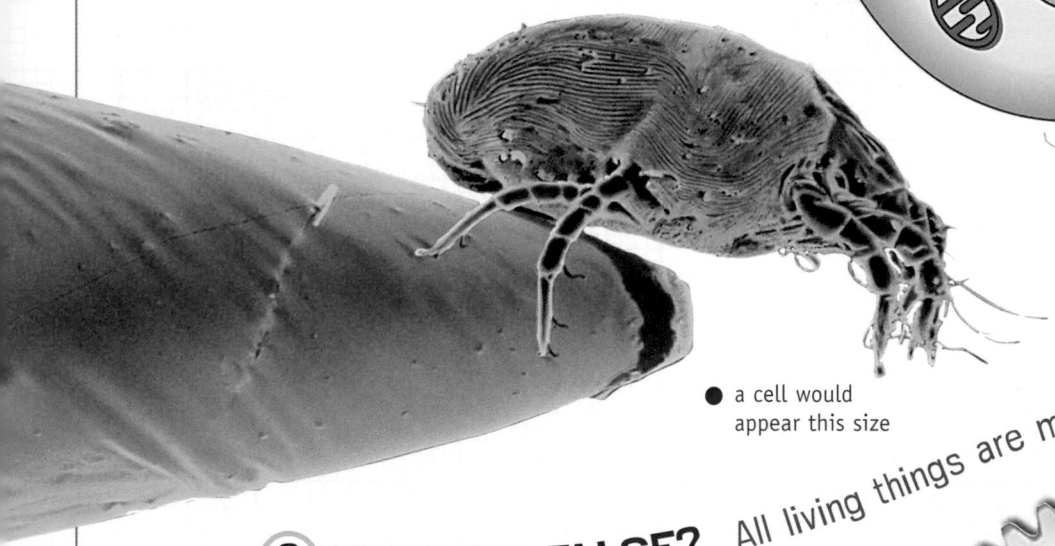

This needle tip and dust mite have been magnified over 400 times

● a cell would appear this size

? TRUE OR FALSE? All living things are made from cells

CELL SIZE

Before the invention of the microscope no one realized that something as small as a cell could exist. To get an idea of the size of a "typical" cell, you can see it here compared to a mite on the the point of a needle. The body's biggest cell, the egg or ovum, is about three times bigger than this, just visible to the naked eye.

DESIGN FEATURES

- Self-reproducing
- Built-in energy supply
- 24/7 service for replacing worn-out cells
- Cell membrane controls imports and exports
- Nucleus contains cell assembly instructions
- Built-in manufacturing, storage, and distribution network
- Available in a wide range of models.

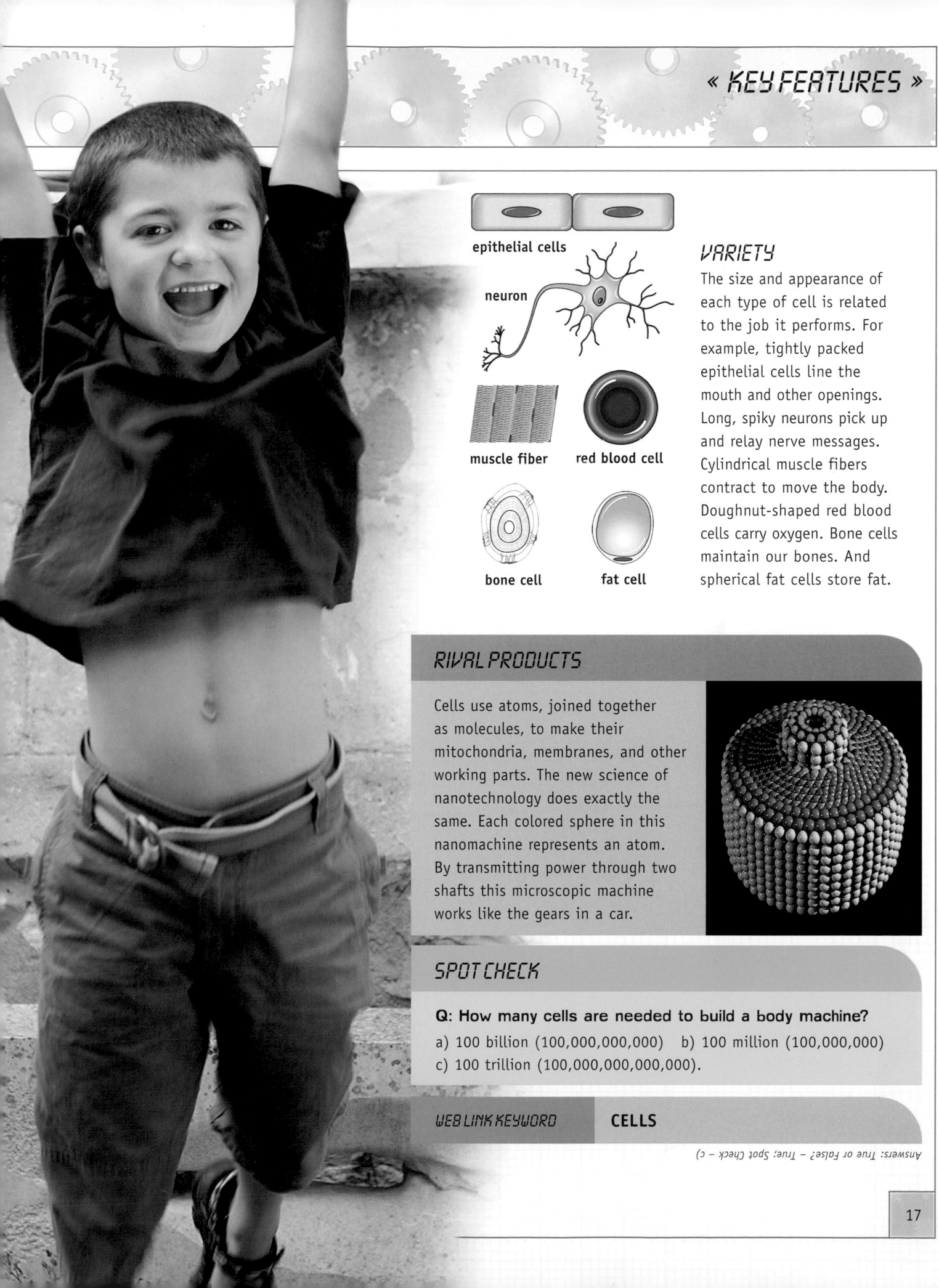

VARIETY

The size and appearance of each type of cell is related to the job it performs. For example, tightly packed epithelial cells line the mouth and other openings. Long, spiky neurons pick up and relay nerve messages. Cylindrical muscle fibers contract to move the body. Doughnut-shaped red blood cells carry oxygen. Bone cells maintain our bones. And spherical fat cells store fat.

RIVAL PRODUCTS

Cells use atoms, joined together as molecules, to make their mitochondria, membranes, and other working parts. The new science of nanotechnology does exactly the same. Each colored sphere in this nanomachine represents an atom. By transmitting power through two shafts this microscopic machine works like the gears in a car.

SPOT CHECK

Q: How many cells are needed to build a body machine?

a) 100 billion (100,000,000,000) b) 100 million (100,000,000)
c) 100 trillion (100,000,000,000,000).

WEB LINK KEYWORD **CELLS**

Answers: True or false? – True; Spot Check – c)

EXTERNAL FEATURES

Separating the human machine's delicate inner workings from the harsh outside world is the skin. This external covering is made of two layers. The outermost, the tough epidermis, is constantly worn away and replaced. The lower, thicker layer, the dermis, contains blood vessels and sensors. Available in a range of colors, skin also provides add-ons, including hairs and nails.

IN THE SWIM

Without skin, we'd lack the protective coat that stops water from getting inside the body, watering down the blood, and disrupting cells. There would be no melanin, the brown coloring that filters out the harmful UV radiation in sunlight. And there would be nothing to stop germs invading deep into every part of the body.

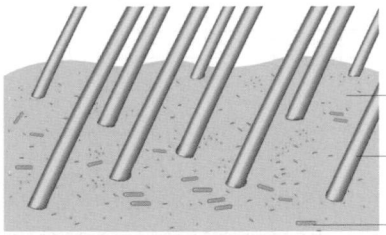

skin helps to stop germs from getting inside the body

TEST YOUR PRODUCT

PINCH TEST

Skin becomes less elastic as we age. Grip a fold of skin on the back of your hand, pull it upward, then release it. It should quickly flatten. Do the same to someone older. Their skin should take longer to flatten.

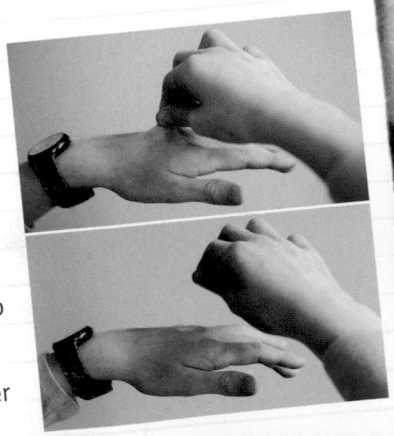

? TRUE OR FALSE?
Fingernails grow faster in summer than winter

exposure to sunlight
can harm the skin

ADDITIONAL DATA

What would we do without nails? These clear, hard coverings that protect the tips of fingers and toes grow from the epidermis, the upper layer of the skin. Fingernails help us to grip objects and pick them up, or to play the guitar. And they're invaluable for scratching annoying itches.

RIVAL PRODUCTS

Insects, including this darkling beetle, belong to a massive group of animals called arthropods. They have a hard outer covering called an exoskeleton. Reptiles have a tough, scaly skin and some, such as this chameleon, can change their skin color to indicate their mood or as camouflage.

SPOT CHECK

Q: How much does an adult's skin weigh?

a) 18oz

b) 4.5lbs or 72oz

c) 11lbs or 176oz

WEB LINK KEYWORD **SKIN**

Answers: True or False? – True; Spot Check – c)

DESIGN FEATURES

- Self-repairing
- Waterproof and germproof
- Filters harmful UV rays in sunshine
- Helps control body temperature
- Full range of touch, heat, cold, and pain sensors
- Produces hairs and nails
- Built-in oil release system keeps surface supple.

LOOK INSIDE

Bones and muscles support and move us; nerves carry the messages that control us and blood delivers the food and oxygen that keeps the body machine's cells working smoothly.

MACHINE INSTRUCTIONS

Stored inside every body cell is the set of instructions to build and operate a human machine. These instructions are called genes. All of us have the same genes—which is why we all appear human. But some genes vary from person to person and give each of us our individual features.

INHERITED FEATURES

From each parent, we inherit a genome, or one set of genes. As a result, you have some of your mother's features and some of your father's. There may be some features that have skipped a generation—your grandparents may have them, but your parents don't. Inherited features, which may run in the family, include red hair, "hitchhiker's" thumb, and the ability—or not—to tongue roll.

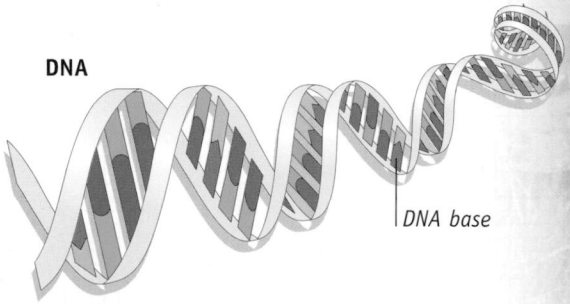

DNA INSTRUCTIONS

Genes are carried in chromosomes, tightly coiled strands made from the chemical DNA. Inside most of your body's cells are 46 chromosomes—23 inherited from your mother and 23 from your father. DNA resembles a twisted ladder, its "rungs" or bases forming the "words" of the instructions.

? TRUE OR FALSE?

Any two humans share 99.9 per cent of their DNA

TEST YOUR PRODUCT
FAMILY TREE

Compare photos of yourself with those of your parents and, if you have any, your brothers and sisters, as well as your grandparents. Can you see any features that have been "passed on" from one generation to the next?

grandparents

parents

child

ADDITIONAL DATA

Because we have two sets of genes, there may be one version of a particular gene in one set, and a different one in the other. For example, take the gene for eye color. If you have one "blue" gene and one "brown" gene, your eyes will probably be brown because the "brown" gene is dominant.

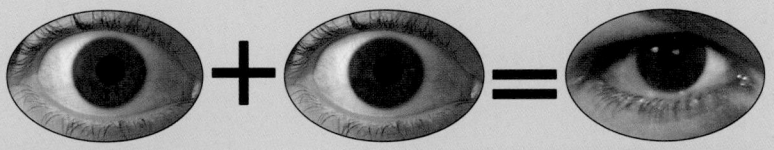

RIVAL PRODUCTS

None—all living things contain DNA.

SPOT CHECK

How many genes are there in a single genome?

a) 250 b) 2,500 c) 25,000.

DESIGN FEATURES

- Two sets of genes inside most cells
- Six and a half feet of DNA packed inside each cell nucleus
- Genes inherited from both parents
- Genes determine appearance of body machine
- Genes are digital instructions encoded in DNA.

WEB LINK KEYWORD **INSTRUCTIONS**

Answers: True or false? – True; Spot Check – c)

BIOMECHANICS

Without its framework of bones, the human machine would collapse in a shapeless heap. Bones create a strong but flexible supporting framework called the skeleton. This is covered by layers of skeletal muscles, so-called because they pull bones to make the body run, jump, and perform many other movements. Muscles also shape the human machine and maintain posture by holding the body upright.

MAKING MOVEMENT

How is this boy able to use his game console? The answer lies in biomechanics, the study of how movement happens. His hands are very flexible because each is made from 27 bones, many with flexible joints between them. Muscles—most extending from his forearm but some in his hand—cross the joints between bones they are attached to and contract (shorten) to make the bones move. These muscles work in a precise order under the control of the brain.

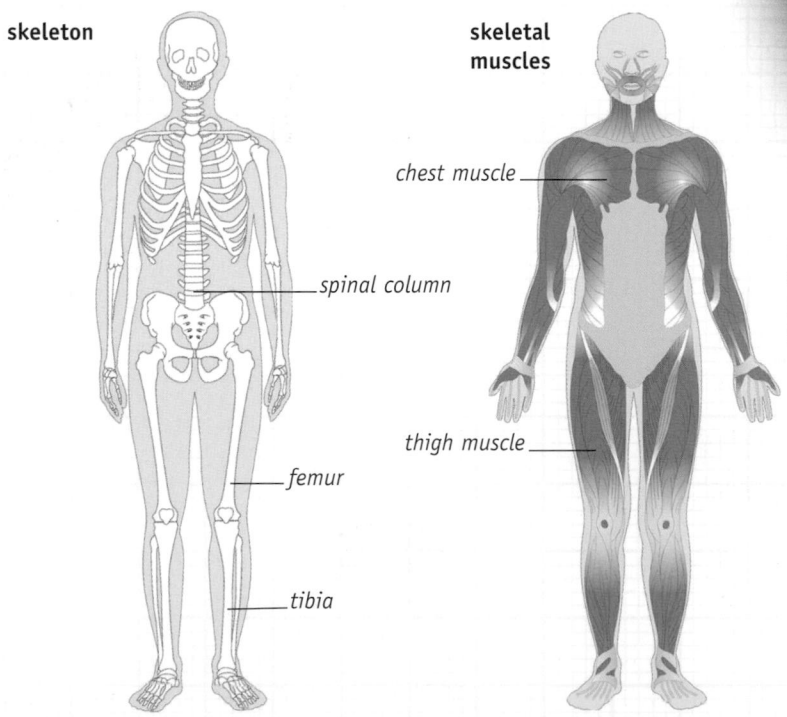

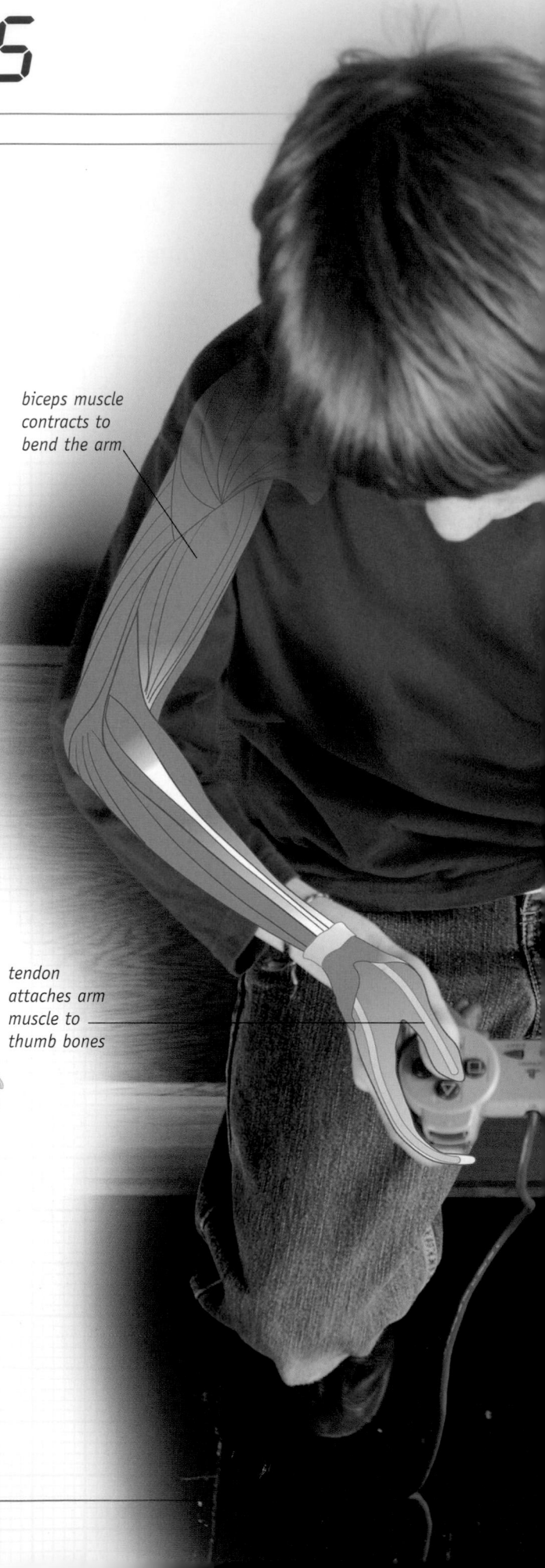

? TRUE OR FALSE?

Muscles can push bones but not pull them

DESIGN FEATURES

- 206-bone skeletal framework
- Bones weight-for-weight six times stronger than steel
- Pulling power of 650 skeletal muscles
- Joints between bones give skeleton flexibility
- Bone self-repair facility
- Flexible, shock-absorbing spinal column.

TEST YOUR PRODUCT

MUSCLE FATIGUE

Make a fist with your fingers. Now open it. Repeat this action as quickly and as many times as you can. Your hand will soon get tired. That's because the muscles that move your body are strong but fatigue (tire) easily.

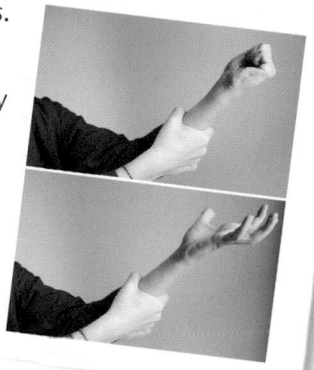

upper arm bone

forearm bone

wrist bone

RIVAL PRODUCTS

Humans are neither the fastest movers on the planet, nor the slowest. While a snail glides slimily at 0.03 mph, an athlete can sprint at up to 22 mph, and a cheetah, the quickest land animal, reaches 62 mph. But the peregrine falcon, the fastest of all animals, can dive at up to 200 mph.

ADDITIONAL DATA

Bones may appear dry and dead but they are not. Day by day, small changes—removing a bit of bone here and adding some there—reshape bones. If you exercise regularly, your bones are reshaped to make them as strong as possible.

SPOT CHECK

Q. Which is the longest bone in your body?

a) Humerus (upper arm bone)

b) Femur (thighbone)

c) Tibia (shinbone).

WEB LINK KEYWORD

BIOMECHANICS

Answers: True or false? – false; Spot Check – b)

WIRING AND COMMUNICATION

Operating the body machine would be impossible without built-in wiring and communications in the form of the nervous system. It is made from billions of interconnected nerve cells, called neurons, that carry electrical signals, called impulses, at lightning speed. The nervous system allows us to feel, to think, and to move.

? TRUE OR FALSE? Nerve cells can last a whole lifetime without being replaced

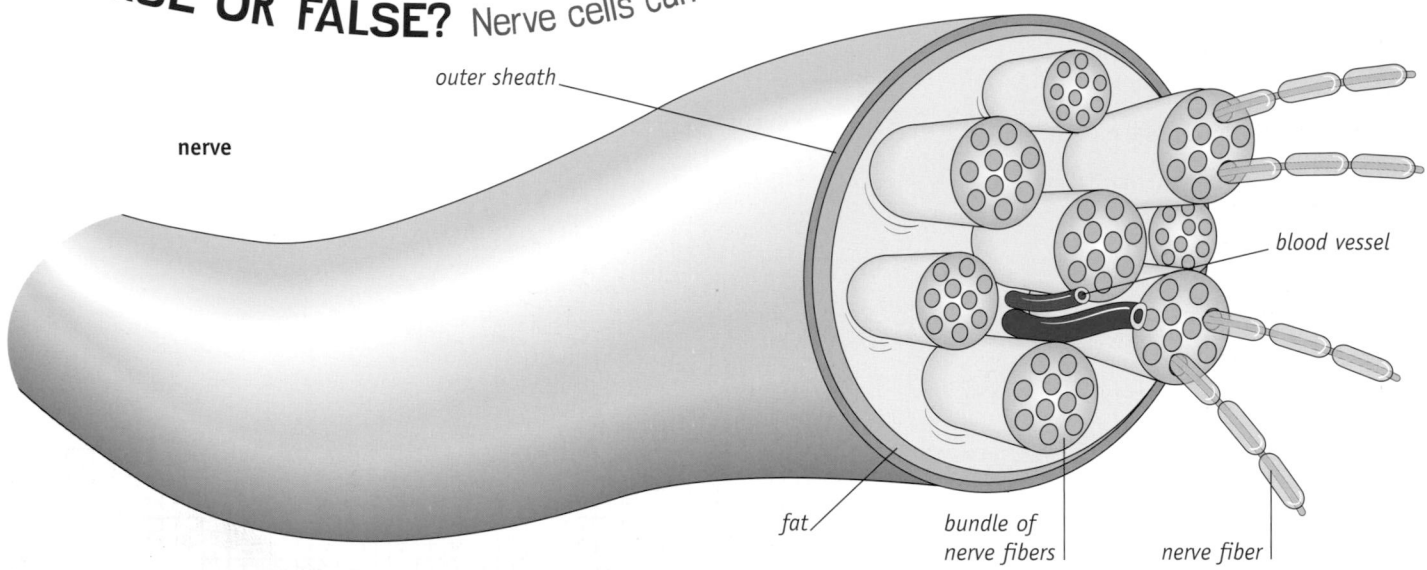

RIVAL PRODUCTS

The Internet is a vast global network of interconnected computers that allows many millions of users to share, receive, and send out information. However, despite the power of this technology, it is still no match for the faster and smarter human brain and nervous system.

NERVE BUNDLES

Nerves are the "cables" that emerge from the brain and spinal cord to relay nerve messages around the body. Each nerve is made up of bundles of nerve fibers, the long impulse-carrying extensions of neurons. The bundles are bound together, along with blood vessels and protective fat, by a protective, bendy sheath.

THE NERVOUS SYSTEM

Controlling and coordinating almost all the body machine's activities is the nervous system. At its core is the central nervous system (CNS)—the brain and spinal cord. Inside the CNS billions of neurons receive information from all parts of the body, process it, and send out instructions. Information is relayed between CNS and all body parts, from toes to teeth, by nerves.

DESIGN FEATURES

- Central information processing unit—the brain
- Multitasking features—sensing, thinking, moving
- Automatic control of body activities
- Spinal cord relay system between brain and body
- High-speed message transfer.

TEST YOUR PRODUCT

REACTION TIMES

You'll need a ruler and a friend. Hold the ruler at the very tip between finger and thumb. Your friend must catch the ruler when you drop it. Note the place on the ruler where it's caught. Now switch. Is your measurement smaller—and reaction time faster?

SPOT CHECK

Q. At what speed do the fastest nerve impulses travel?

a) 217 mph b) 21.7 mph c) 2.2 mph.

WEB LINK KEYWORD **WIRING**

Answers: True or False? – True; Spot Check – a)

INTERNAL TRANSPORT

The trillions of cells that make up the body machine need to be nurtured constantly to avoid system malfunctions. Nonstop care and attention is provided by the body's internal transport network, the circulatory system. Blood, pumped by the heart along tubes called blood vessels, carries oxygen, food, warmth, and other essentials to cells and removes their wastes for disposal.

CIRCULATORY SYSTEM

Blood is pumped around the body through two loops. The heart has two sides, each with an upper atrium and lower ventricle. Oxygen-depleted blood (blue) from the body enters the right atrium, and is pumped by the right ventricle to the lungs to pick up oxygen before returning to the left atrium. The left ventricle pumps oxygen-rich blood (red) to the body's oxygen-hungry cells. Arteries carry blood away from the heart, veins toward the heart. Tiny vessels called capillaries link arteries and veins.

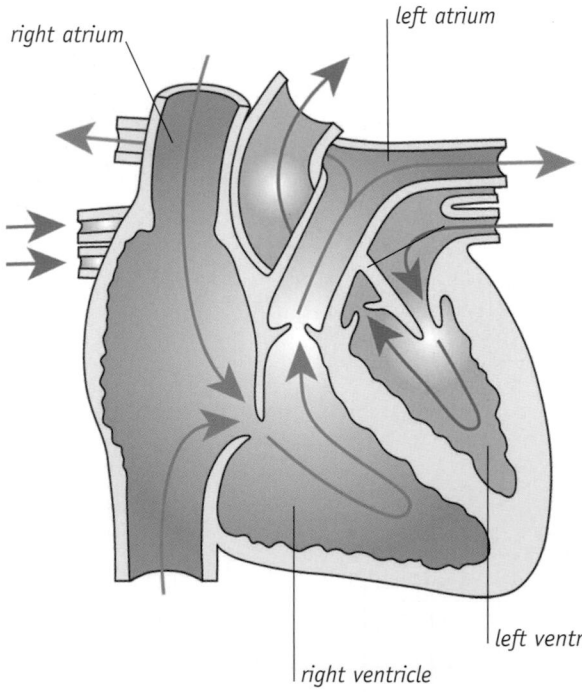

circulatory system

capillaries
arteries to head and arms
veins to heart
arteries to lungs
veins from lungs
veins from lungs
arteries to liver
veins to heart
arteries to stomach and intestines
vein to liver
arteries to legs
capillaries

? TRUE OR FALSE?

Stretched out, your blood vessels would stretch around the world four times

DESIGN FEATURES

- Blood vessel network reaches all parts of the body
- Every cell has dedicated delivery service provided by capillaries
- Blood delivers essentials to cells and removes wastes
- Heart works constantly without tiring.

TEST YOUR PRODUCT

MEASURING HEART RATE

Do this by feeling your pulse, the surge of blood along an artery every time your heart beats. Put two fingers on your wrist and count the number of pulses for a minute. That is your heart rate. Do the same after exercise. Your heart rate increases to get extra oxygen to your muscles.

BLOOD

About 10.5 pints of this red liquid flow through blood vessels. Blood consists of oxygen-carrying red blood cells, which give blood its color, and a yellow fluid called plasma in which float white blood cells. These defend the body against disease. Plasma carries food and chemical messengers called hormones along with waste produced by body cells. Blood also distributes heat around the body.

RIVAL PRODUCTS

This lightweight pump (below right) can be attached to a severely damaged heart to help it work properly. Artificial blood (below left) has been developed by scientists for people who have lost blood; it can be used with any blood group and is disease-free.

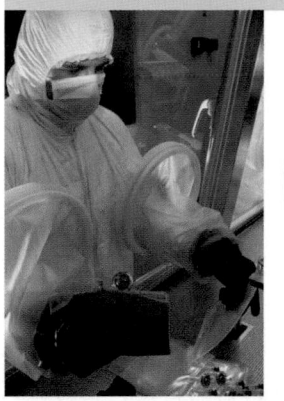

TOP TIP

Good health depends on keeping the circulatory system working at its best. This means getting regular exercise, and eating a varied diet with little fat or salt.

SPOT CHECK

When we are resting, our hearts beat on average:

a) 25 times per minute
b) 75 times per minute
c) 125 times per minute.

WEB LINK KEYWORD **CIRCULATION**

Answers: True or false? – True; Spot Check – b)

AUTOMATIC OPERATIONS

Controlling how much light enters our eyes is just one of many of the human machine's automatic functions. These enable the body to run itself, giving us the freedom to sense, to think, and to communicate.

VENTILATION

Oxygen, one of the gases in the air around us, is key to the body's operations. Our cells use it to release the energy stored in glucose, which we get from food, and this drives body processes. Releasing energy also produces a poisonous waste called carbon dioxide. Breathing, or ventilation, gets oxygen into the body and gets rid of carbon dioxide.

BREATHING AIR

The business of breathing revolves around the two spongy lungs that fill most of the space in your chest. Air travels to the lungs through the nose—where it is warmed and cleaned—throat, and trachea (windpipe), which branches into left and right bronchi. Movements of the ribs and diaphragm—a sheet of muscle underneath the lungs—breathes air into, and out of, the lungs.

? TRUE OR FALSE?

There are over 300 million alveoli in your two lungs

RIVAL PRODUCTS

Not all animals use lungs to breathe. Earthworms take in oxygen from the air through their moist surface. Insects, such as this praying mantis, breathe through small holes that pipe air around the body. Fish get oxygen from the water they swim in through their gills.

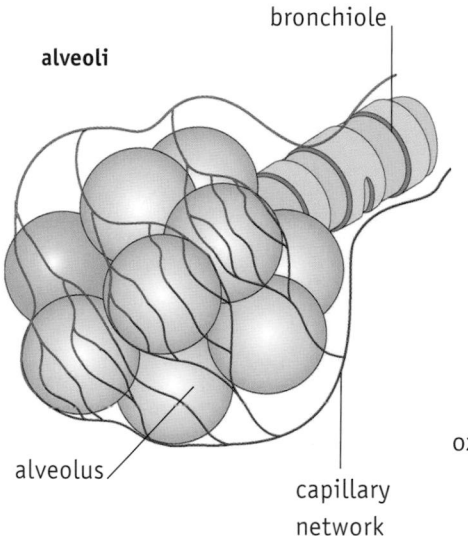

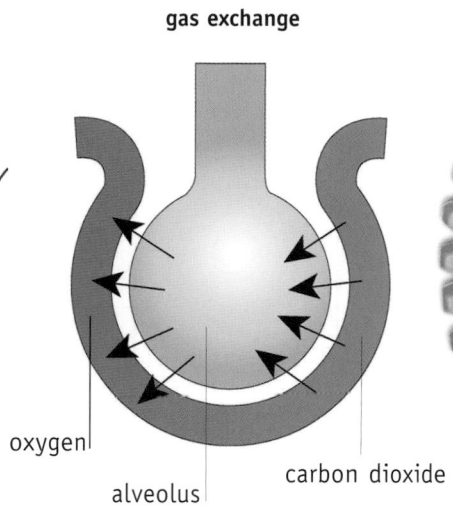

DESIGN FEATURES

- Built-in nasal air filter
- Automatic ventilation mechanism
- Tennis-court-sized surface for taking in oxygen packed inside chest
- Automatic adjustment of breathing rate during exercise
- Flexible ducting links lungs to nose
- 24/7 expulsion of waste carbon dioxide.

EXCHANGING GASES

The lung's bronchi branch into smaller and smaller branches, eventually becoming tiny bronchioles no wider than a hair that end in bunches of rounded air bags. Enclosed by blood capillaries, these alveoli provide a massive surface for exchanging gases. Oxygen from breathed-in air passes from the alveolus into the bloodstream to be carried away to cells. Carbon dioxide moves in the opposite direction to be breathed out.

ADDITIONAL DATA

Smoking cigarettes damages the lungs and the rest of the breathing system. Cigarette smoke contains chemicals that can cause cancer. Smoking makes people unfit and short of breath. Over time it also ages the skin prematurely.

TEST YOUR PRODUCT
CATCH YOUR BREATH

Breathe onto a mirror, or a pane of glass, to see what happens. It should mist up because the air you breathe out has been warmed and moistened while inside your lungs. On the cool glass surface, water vapor in the breathed-out air condenses to produce a fine mist.

SPOT CHECK

Q. What percentage of the air is made up by oxygen?

a) 1%
b) 21%
c) 91%.

WEB LINK KEYWORD **VENTILATION**

Answers: True or False? – True; Spot Check – b)

REFUELING

Eating food every day is essential to refuel the human machine and keep it working. The nutrients in food supply energy to power the body's activities as well as the raw materials needed for growth and repair. But these nutrients are "locked" inside big molecules. These have to be broken down into smaller nutrient molecules that can be used by our cells.

BREAKING DOWN

In many factories, products are made by fitting together different components. In the human machine, digestion—breaking down food into its basic parts—works in the opposite direction. Mechanical digestion—being crushed by the teeth or churned by the muscular wall of the stomach—turns solid food into a thick soup. Chemical digesters called enzymes also get to work. They split big molecules into smaller ones that can be absorbed into the bloodstream.

DESIGN FEATURES

- Automatic swallowing
- Built-in chop and crush feature
- Hunger feature automatically signals need for refueling
- Range of enzymes to digest different foods
- Automatic release of digestive juices at mealtimes
- Long intestines for efficient digestion and absorption
- Regular emptying of waste.

TEST YOUR PRODUCT
STARCH TO SUGAR

You'll need a piece of white bread. Put it in your mouth and chew it for two minutes. Notice how the taste changes. It should taste bland at first, then sweet. That's because an enzyme in saliva (spit) digests bland-tasting starch in bread into sweet-tasting sugars.

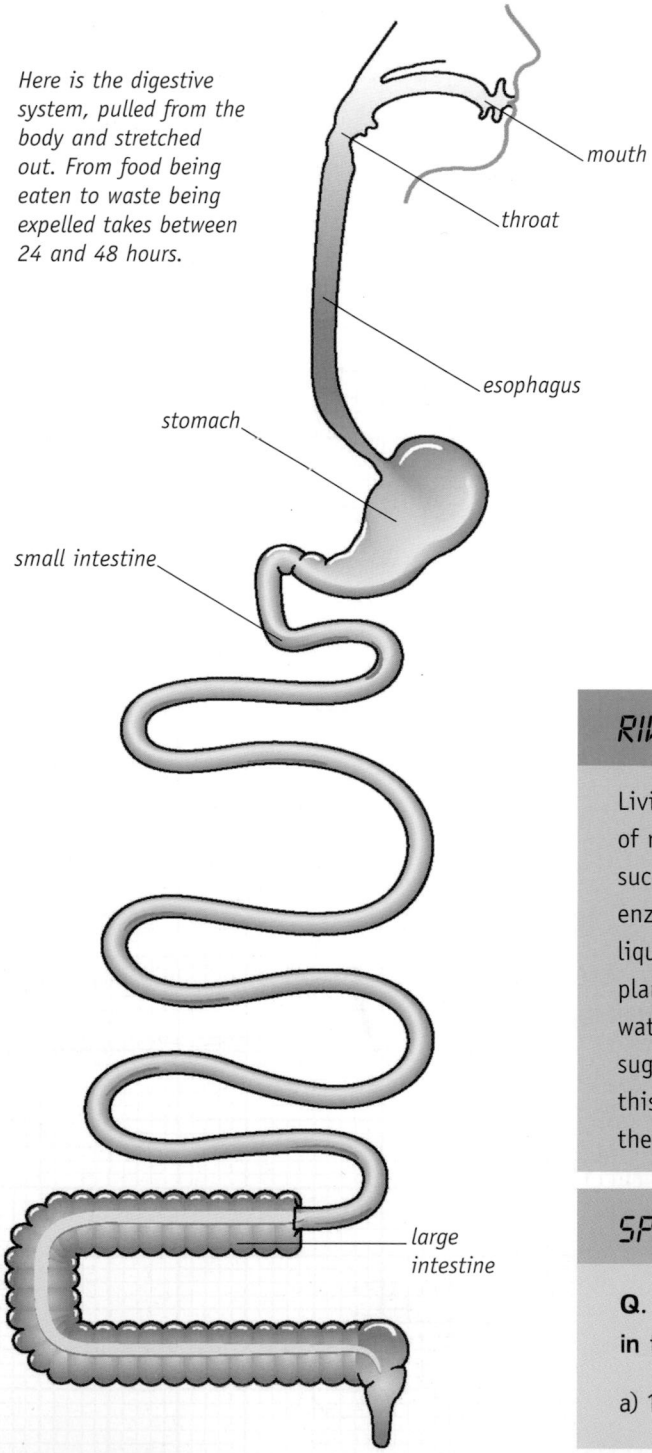

Here is the digestive system, pulled from the body and stretched out. From food being eaten to waste being expelled takes between 24 and 48 hours.

? TRUE OR FALSE?

An average person eats 27.2 tons of food in a lifetime

DIGESTIVE SYSTEM

This consists of a tube—some 29.5 feet long—that extends downward from the mouth. After the food is chewed in the mouth and swallowed, it is pushed down the esophagus to the stomach. Here it is pummeled into a soup and part digested. In the small intestine, enzymes complete digestion and nutrients are absorbed into the bloodstream and carried to hungry body cells. Any undigested food passes along the large intestine and is expelled to the outside.

RIVAL PRODUCTS

Living things display a range of refueling techniques. Fungi, such as bread mold, release enzymes, then absorb the liquid remains. Trees and other plants use sunshine to convert water and carbon dioxide into sugars. Some animals, such as this mosquito (right), feed on the blood of other animals.

SPOT CHECK

Q. How many teeth do adults have in their upper and lower jaws?

a) 16 + 16 b) 10 + 10 c) 14 + 18.

WEB LINK KEYWORD **FUEL**

Answers: True or false? – True; Spot Check – a)

ONBOARD COMPUTER

The most complex organ in the known universe, the brain is the human machine's onboard computer. It is responsible for routine sensory operations, such as seeing outside, and control functions, such as regulating heartbeat. But it also gives us personality, sends us to sleep, makes us think, gets us angry, and tells the body how to move.

? TRUE OR FALSE?

If it could be touched the brain would feel like thick, warm oatmeal

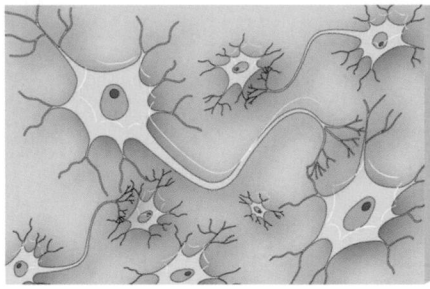

neurons

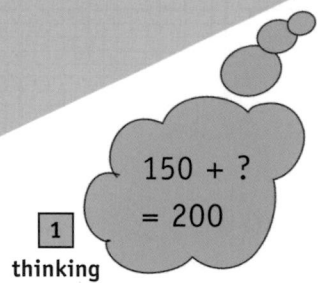

1 thinking

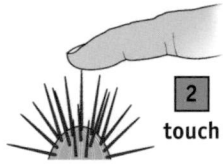

2 touch

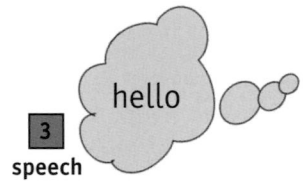

3 speech

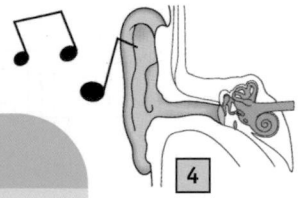

4 hearing

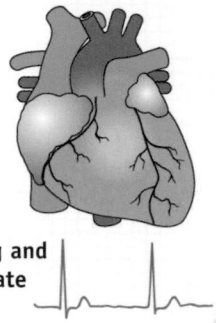

5 breathing and heart rate

BRAIN AREAS

The brain has three main parts. The cerebellum makes us move smoothly and stand up straight. The brain stem controls heart rate and links the brain to the spinal cord and the rest of the body. The cerebrum, the biggest part, has a surface layer packed with neurons (nerve cells). It is divided into different areas that control different aspects of our behavior, such as speech, touch, vision, hearing, movement, and thinking.

SPOT CHECK

Q. The brain makes up two percent of the body's total weight but uses how much of its energy?

a) 2%

b) 10%

c) 20%.

DESIGN FEATURES

- Network of 100 billion neurons
- Over 100 trillion connections between neurons in the network
- Sensory inputs from all parts of the body
- Control outputs to muscles and glands
- Customized bony protective skull case
- Memory storage capacity of 100,000 gigabytes.

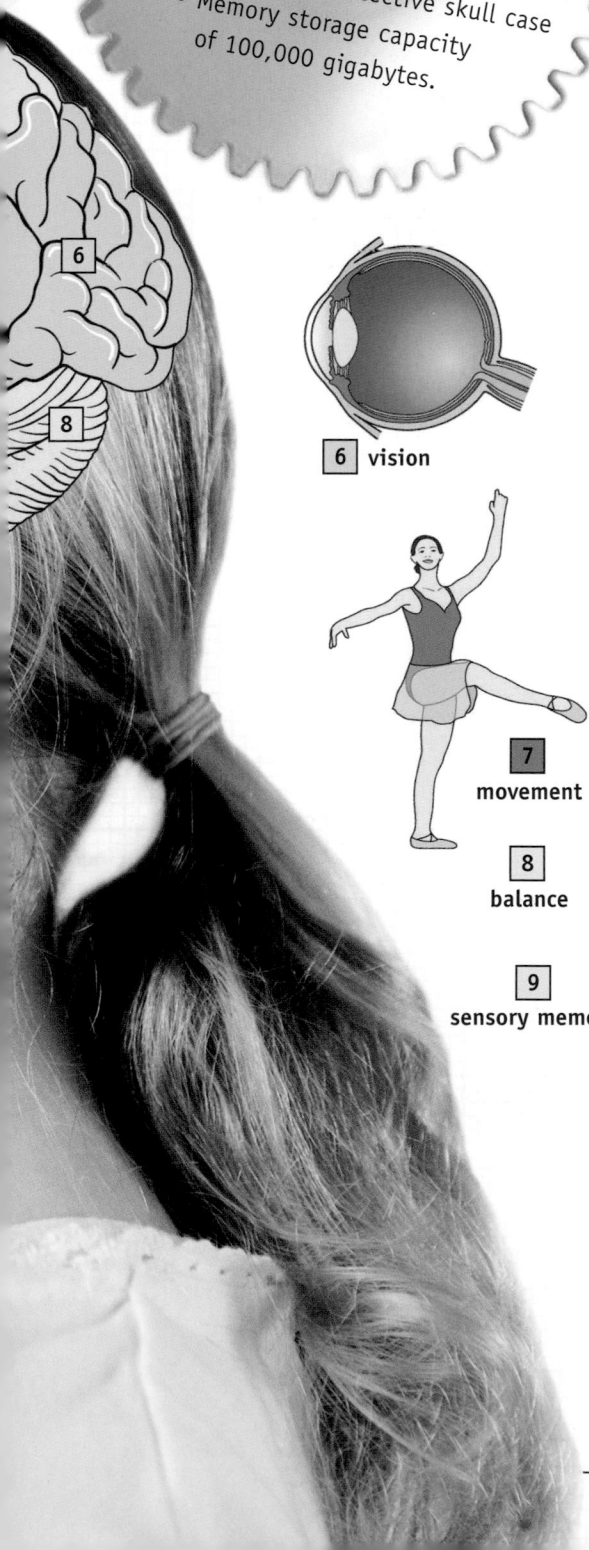

ADDITIONAL DATA

The cerebrum has left and right halves called hemispheres that are connected. The left hemisphere controls the right side of the body. It also deals with math, spoken and written language, and problem solving. The right hemisphere controls the left side of the body. It also deals with creativity, humor, music, and recognizing faces.

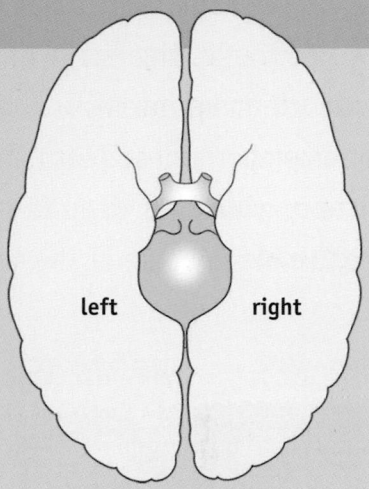

RIVAL PRODUCTS

A single ant's brain may be tiny, but the collective brain power of a colony of these social insects allows it to act as a superorganism. As computer chips get smaller and more powerful, computers are able to perform increasingly difficult tasks. But as yet, no computer matches the human brain in terms of complexity and versatility.

TOP TIP

Reading, solving crosswords, playing chess, and brainteasers like this one are all great ways of improving brain fitness.

Move just three matches to convert three triangles into five. (Answer on page 73)

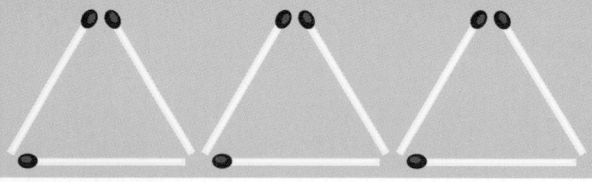

WEB LINK KEYWORD **COMPUTER**

Answers: True or False? – True; Spot Check – c)

PREPROGRAMMED FEATURES

The brain is equipped with special built-in features. Some make life less hazardous, others make life more interesting, while others enable us to remember and to learn. In charge is the limbic system, which lies deep in the cerebrum, the "thinking" part of the brain.

limbic system

cerebrum *thalamus* *amygdala*

hippocampus

SADNESS HAPPINESS

MEMORY

GETTING EMOTIONAL

Key parts of the limbic system include the amygdala, which produces fear, and the hippocampus, which is central to memory. The thalamus relays incoming information from the brain stem and spinal cord. Overall, the limbic system controls emotions, such as sadness and happiness. And, if a special smell brings back a memory, that's the limbic system at work.

DESIGN FEATURES

- Limbic system controls built-in emotions
- Fear function protects human machine against threats
- Emotions make life more interesting
- Massive memory storage facility
- Learning module active throughout life.

REMEMBER AND LEARN

Facts, faces, events, skills...The human brain has an incredible facility to remember things. We retain some memories for just a short time and then discard them. More important ones are shuttled repeatedly between the hippocampus and cerebrum until they are filed in long-term memory. Long-term memory plays a crucial role in learning, from a child's first steps to understanding a foreign language.

TEST YOUR PRODUCT

MEMORY TEST

Ask a friend to collect 20 different objects. Take two minutes to look at the objects and memorize them. Then ask them, in your absence, to hide five of the objects. On your return, can you name all five? Repeat the test and see if you can improve your memory.

? TRUE OR FALSE?

Fear of phobias is called phobophobia

RIVAL PRODUCTS

A frightened cat automatically stands tall to make itself look bigger and more threatening as part of a preprogrammed response to enemies. In the African savanna, wildebeest have a built-in system that makes them migrate at the same time each year to find new feeding grounds and sources of water.

ADDITIONAL DATA

Fear is important because it can alert us to dangerous situations. Some people, however, develop phobias to certain objects and situations. A phobia is an irrational fear of something that is usually harmless, such as this spider.

SPOT CHECK

Q. Which of these words describes an irrational fear of spiders?

a) Ailurophobia
b) Arachnophobia
c) Apiphobia.

WEB LINK KEYWORD	MEMORY

Answers: True or false? – True; Spot Check – b) [a) is cats, c) is bees]

SHUTDOWN MODE

We know that sleep is vitally important to all of us because without it we feel tired and ill. Each evening a natural mechanism built into the brain gradually reduces its activity so we go from being wide awake to feeling sleepy. Each morning the reverse happens and we wake up. During sleep the body has a chance to rest, while the brain has time to sort and process the previous day's experiences.

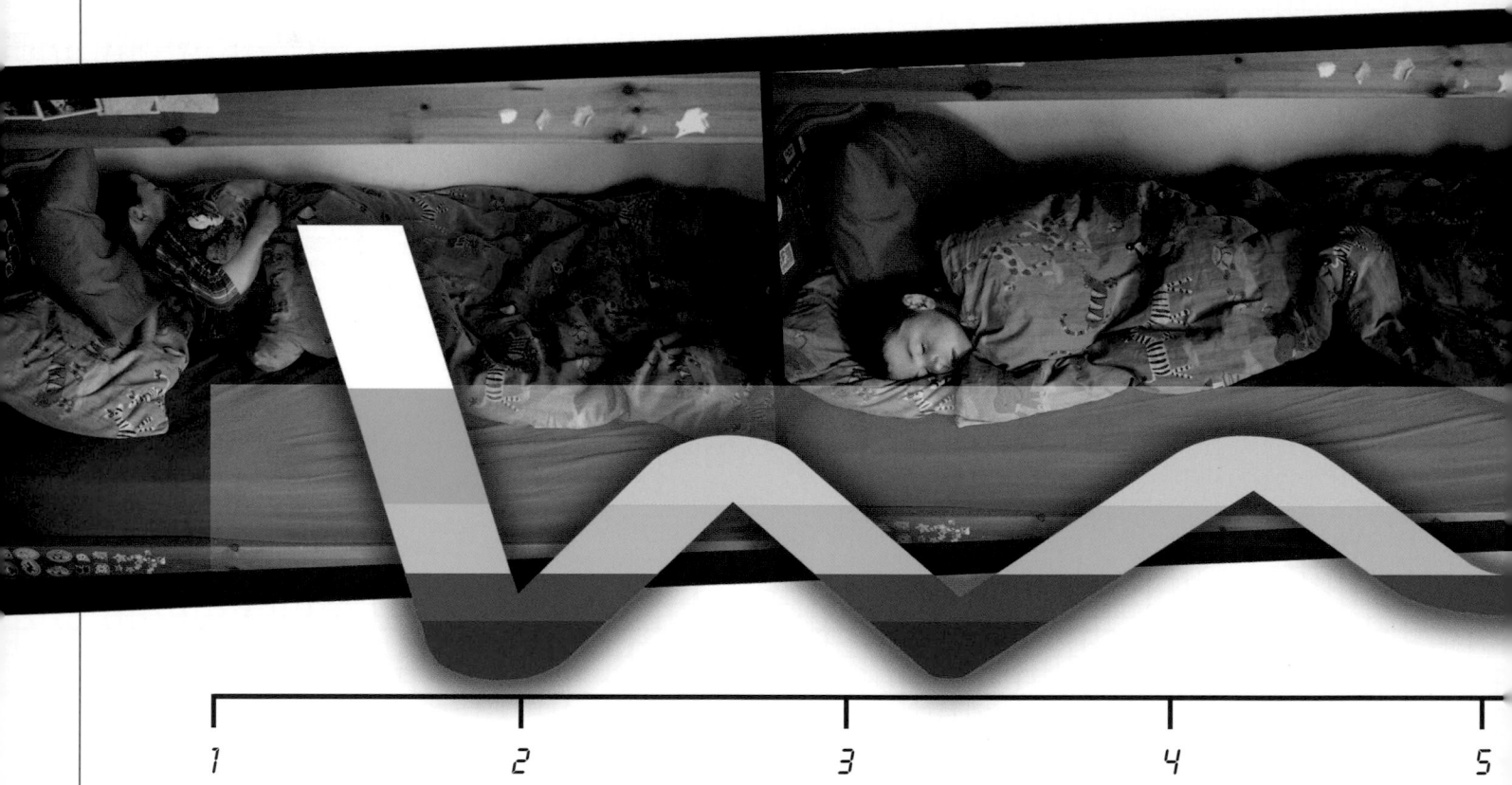

SLEEP PATTERNS

Each night, two types of sleep follow each other repeatedly, as shown by this graph. We doze off and slip through stages of NREM (nonrapid eye movement) sleep into deep sleep. This is followed by lighter REM (rapid eye movement) sleep, when the body, apart from the eyes, cannot move.

DREAMS

Many scientists think dreams are produced when the brain "replays" daily experiences so that they get shunted into permanent, long-term memory. Dreams are played out mainly during REM sleep.

RIVAL PRODUCTS

Koalas snooze for 20 hours a day to save energy. Migrating birds, such as swifts, take lots of short naps in the air. Dolphins sleep with only one half of the brain "switched off" to make sure they don't drown.

DESIGN FEATURES

- Automatic nighttime shutdown facility triggers sleep
- Automatic decrease in breathing, heart rate, and body temperature
- Emergency wake-up mode when "things go bump in the night"
- Endless variety of dreams available
- Optional snoring feature
- Automatic daytime wake-up mechanism ends sleep.

? TRUE OR FALSE?

In all, people spend around one-third of their lives asleep

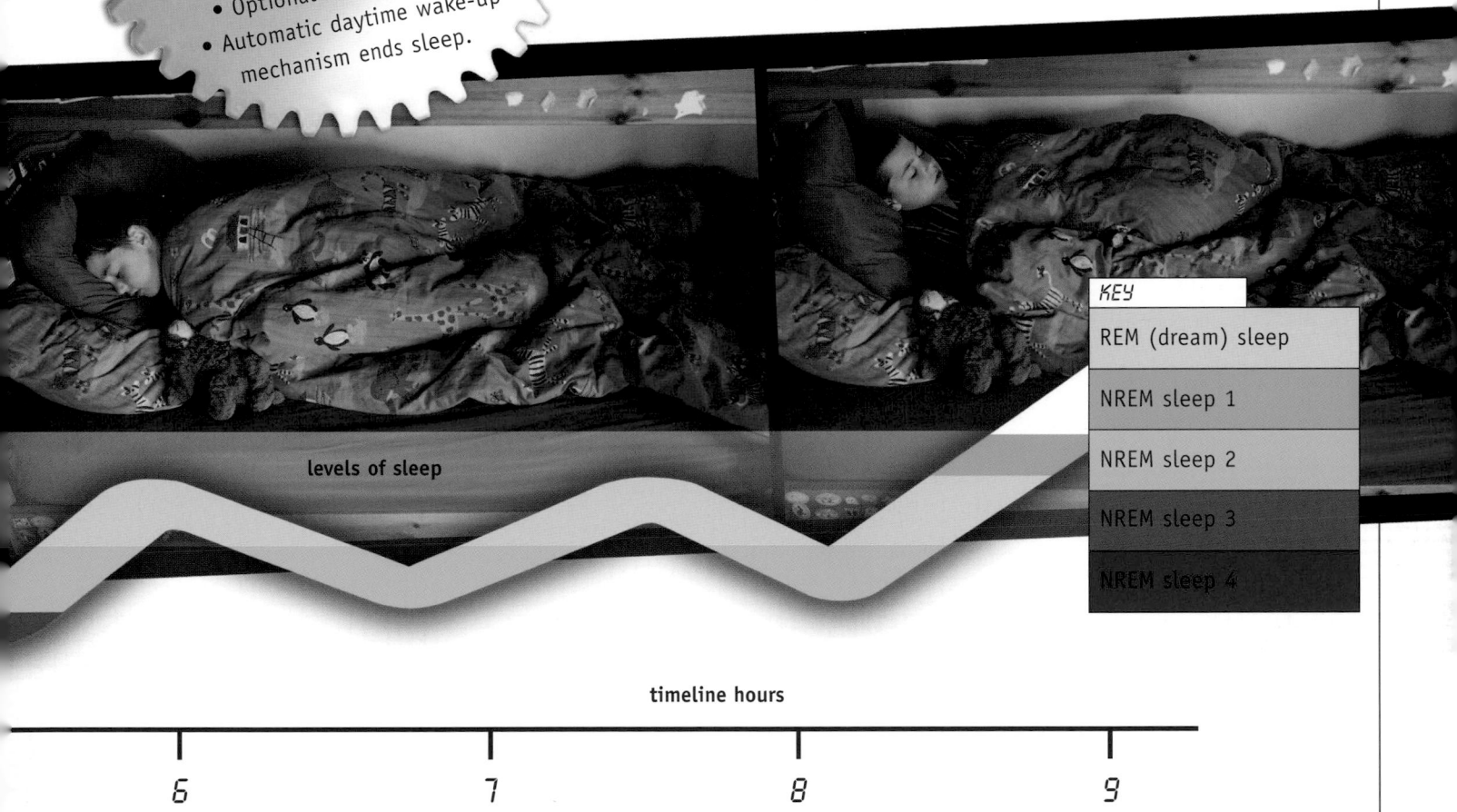

ADDITIONAL DATA

This sleeping man's head is "wired up" to an EEG machine. This detects and displays "brainwaves," the patterns of electrical activity produced by his brain cells. Brainwave activity is much "busier" during REM sleep than deep sleep.

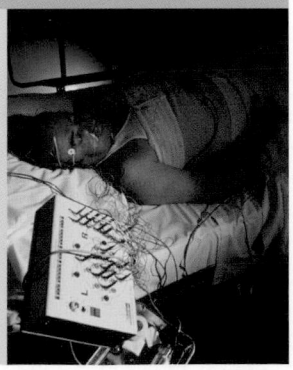

SPOT CHECK

Q. How many hours' sleep does the average young adult need?

a) Seven hours
b) Nine hours
c) Five hours.

WEB LINK KEYWORD **SLEEP**

Answers: True or false? – True; Spot Check – b)

ENVIRONMENTAL SENSORS

In order to operate, the body machine has to sense and react to changes in its surroundings or environment. The smell of smoke, for example, can alert it to danger, while the taste of ice cream can provide enjoyment. A battery of sensors detect stimuli—changes—and send messages to the brain, which interprets and responds to them.

DESIGN FEATURES

- Millions of smell sensors in the nasal cavity inside the nose
- Versatile skin sensors that detect touch, pressure, vibration, heat, cold, and pain
- Hands and lips most sensitive parts of skin
- Ten thousand taste buds in the tongue
- Ears detect pitch, loudness, and direction of sound.

? TRUE OR FALSE?

The human nose can distinguish over 10,000 different smells

RIVAL PRODUCTS

Some animals can sense things we cannot. Rattlesnakes can "see" the heat given off by prey at night with sensors that detect infrared radiation. Honeybees can detect patterns in flower petals that are invisible to us because they can "see" ultraviolet light. And bats use ultrasound, too high-pitched for us to hear, to navigate and catch insect prey.

THE SENSES

Sensors give us our senses—taste, touch, hearing, and smell. The fifth, vision, is so important that it has its own pages (46–47). Taste buds in the tongue detect sweet, sour, salt, bitter, and umami (meaty) tastes. Millions of skin sensors allow us to feel objects. Sensors deep inside the ear detect sounds. And smell sensors high up in the nose enable us to smell flowers, enjoy food, and avoid danger.

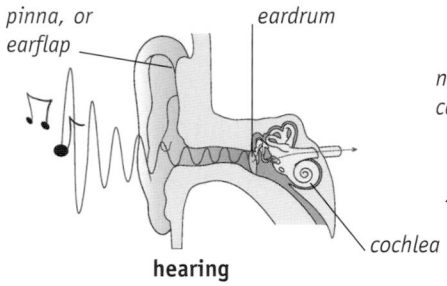

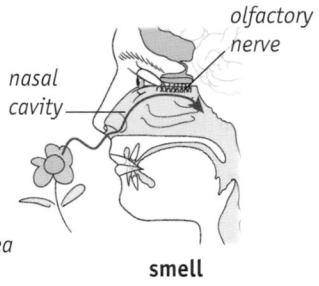

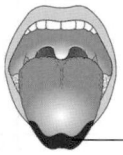

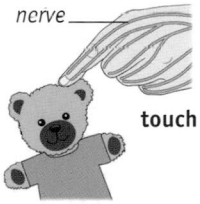

TEST YOUR PRODUCT

TASTE TEST

You will need a friend, a blindfold, a nose clip, and several different types of food, such as pretzels, chocolate, and apple, cut into small pieces. Blindfolded and with a nose clip, how many food items can your friend identify by taste alone? Probably not many.

SPOT CHECK

Q. The loudness of sounds is measured in

a) Decapods

b) Megabytes

c) Decibels.

Answers: True or False? – True; Spot Check – c)

WEB LINK KEYWORD **SENSORS**

VISUAL DISPLAY UNIT

Of all the body's senses, vision is the most important. It allows the human machine to interact with and navigate around its surroundings. The sense organs that make vision possible are the two eyes, housed in protective sockets in the front of the skull. They contain millions of light-detecting sensors that send messages to the brain.

SEEING IN ACTION

Light reflected from an outside object passes through the cornea, the clear part of the eye, and through the pupil. The cornea focuses the light, as does the clear lens, to produce a sharp, upside-down image of the skateboarder on the retina. This layer of light sensors covering the inside of the eye sends messages along the optic nerve to the back of the brain. Here, in the visual area, those signals are turned into pictures that you can "see."

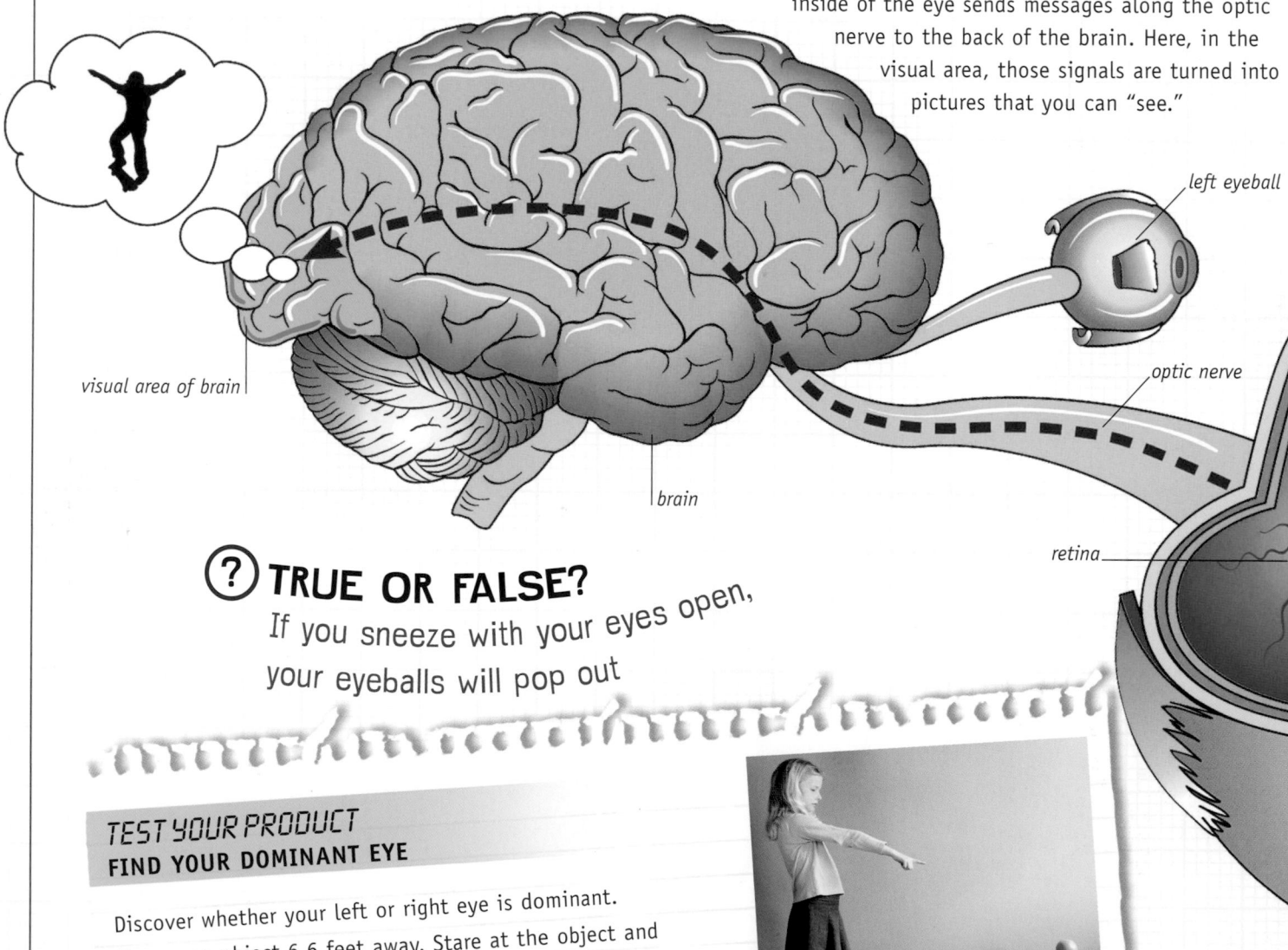

? TRUE OR FALSE?

If you sneeze with your eyes open, your eyeballs will pop out

TEST YOUR PRODUCT
FIND YOUR DOMINANT EYE

Discover whether your left or right eye is dominant. Choose an object 6.6 feet away. Stare at the object and point at it, using an index finger—you will see two blurry fingers. Close each eye in turn. When your dominant eye is open, your finger will point directly at the object.

DESIGN FEATURES

- Blink and wipe-clean function
- Automatic light-level control
- Multidirectional in-socket movement
- Automatic focusing
- Analogue-digital conversion
- Full color operation on most models
- High-speed link to brain via optic nerve.

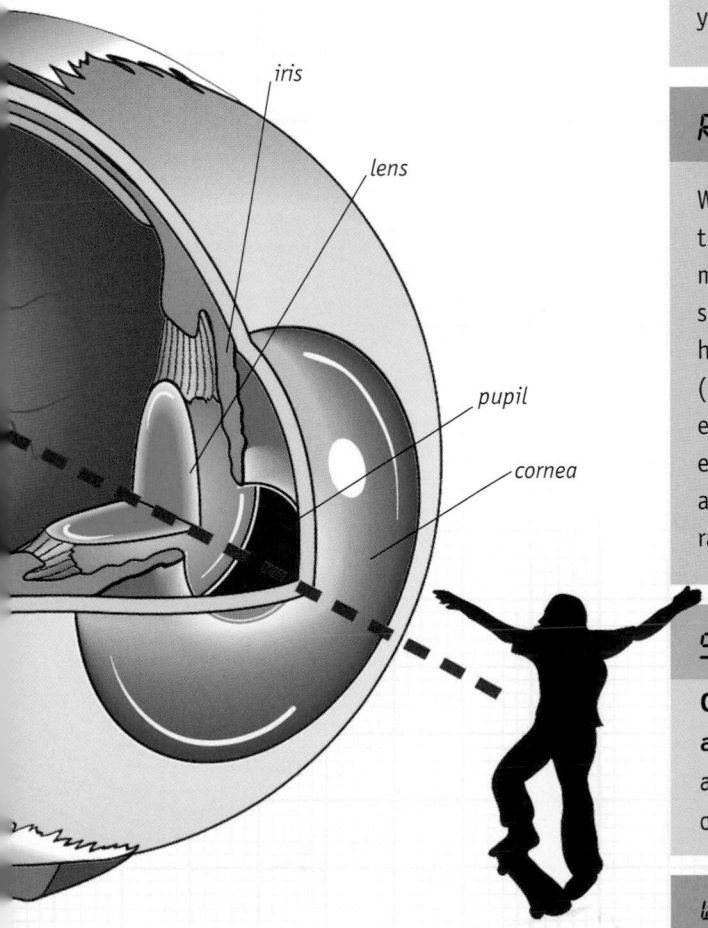

ADDITIONAL DATA

How much light enters the eye is controlled automatically by the iris, the colored part of the eye. In dim light, the iris makes the pupil wider (top). More light enters the eye so you can see more clearly. In bright light, it makes the pupil—the black hole at its center—narrower (bottom) so you are not dazzled.

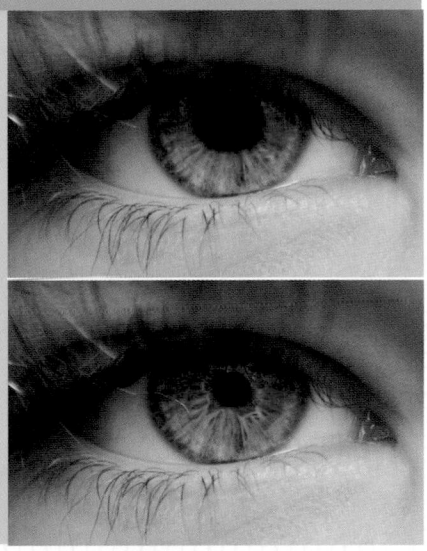

RIVAL PRODUCTS

With its single lens, the eye of the squid (top), and other top mollusks, like the octopus, is surprisingly similar to the human eye. The insect eye (bottom)—called a compound eye—is made of many units, each with its own lens. It has an amazing ability to detect rapid movement.

SPOT CHECK

Q. Over what distance can the human eye detect a lighted candle at night?

a) 328 feet away b) 3,281 feet (0.62 miles) away

c) 32,810 feet (6.2 miles) away.

WEB LINK KEYWORD **VISION**

Answers: True or false? – false; Spot Check – b)

OPTICAL TESTS

Throughout the day, your brain has to make sense of the constant stream of signals it receives from your eyes. It uses a wide range of visual clues to work out the identity, shape, size, color, and other features of the scene before you. But the human machine isn't foolproof. The brain can be tricked into seeing things that aren't the same way in reality. You can test this out with the optical illusions on these pages.

SEEING THINGS

Sometimes the brain adds things that aren't there. The white triangle (below) doesn't really exist. Your brain created it using remembered information. The gray "dots" that appear in the grid (right) are produced when sensors in the eye send confused signals to the brain.

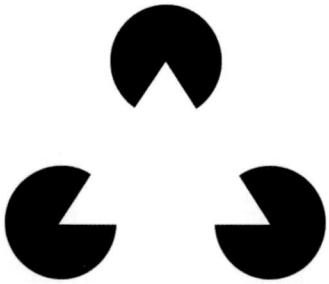

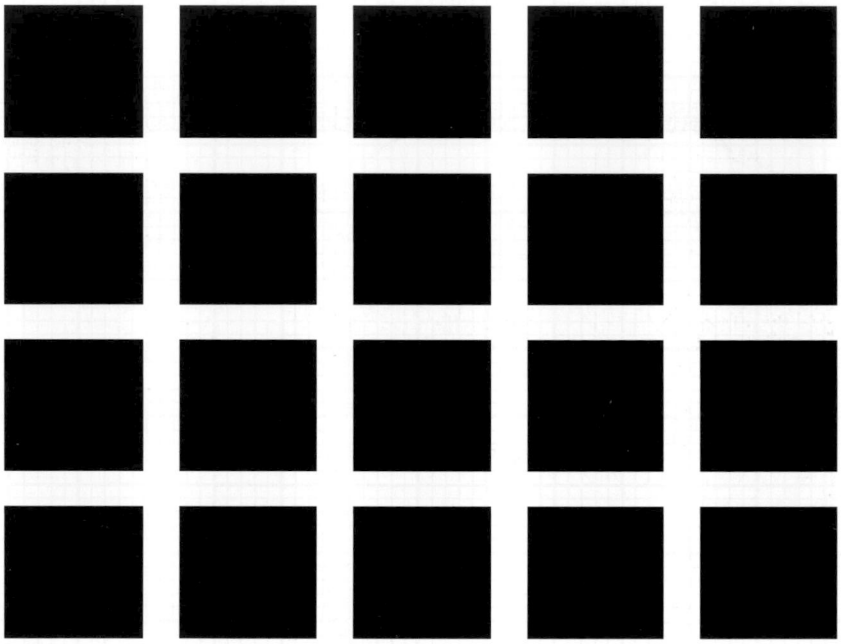

DIFFERENT SIZES?

The brain calculates the size of an object with the help of clues in the background. If those clues are confusing, the brain can be easily misled. Here, the sloping lines create the illusion that the girl on the right is bigger than the one on the left. Check them with a ruler—they are all the same size.

? TRUE OR FALSE? Both eyes "see" exactly the same view of the outside world

COLOR CONFUSION

Look at the two groups of red squares. At first glance, the top group appears to be a different shade from the bottom group. In fact, they're identical. The different colored bars, however, fool the brain into thinking that the squares are not the same shade.

DESIGN FEATURES

- Brain fills gaps when there is insufficient information from eyes
- Faces only recognized by brain if seen the right way up
- Brain judges an object's shape according to its background
- Brain judges an object's size according to its background
- Brain judges an object's color by its surroundings.

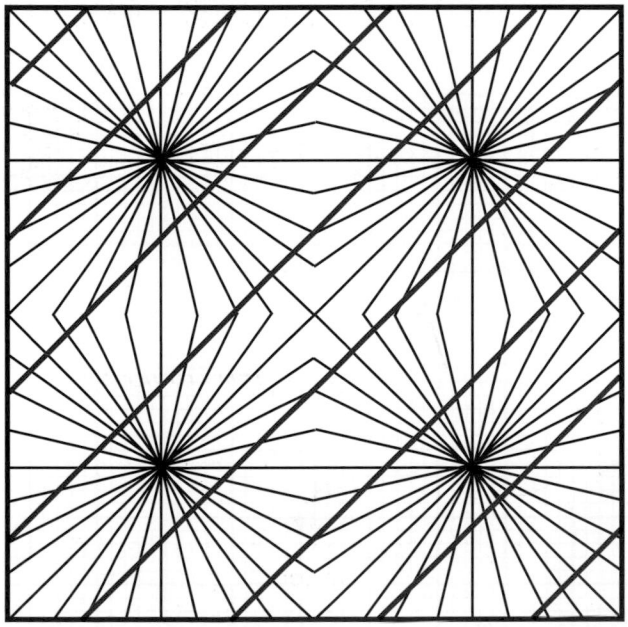

STRAIGHT OR CURVED

Believe it or not, every line in this image is a straight line. The background pattern of black lines distorts the diagonal red lines so that they appear curved. To check this, take a ruler and hold its edge against one of the red lines.

SPOT CHECK

Q. Which part of your brain analyzes signals from the eyes so you can see?

a) Front b) Top c) Back.

WEB LINK KEYWORD **TESTS**

Answers: True or false? – false; Spot Check – c)

COMMUNICATION SYSTEMS

We humans are social beings who enjoy and need company. Communication plays a key role in the way we live because, for example, it enables us to make friends and show how we feel. The ways by which we communicate include body language and facial expressions. But by far the most powerful communication tool is unique to humans—speech enables us to pass on ideas, thoughts, and intentions to one or many people.

SENDING MESSAGES

You can tell how someone feels by facial expressions (left), such as smiling and frowning. These are produced by over 30 small muscles that pull on the skin of the face. Body language (top right), such as these aggressive/defensive postures, clearly reveal a person's intentions and thoughts. New methods of communication (top left) include e-mail and websites.

? TRUE OR FALSE? It takes more muscles to frown than to smile

RIVAL PRODUCTS

Animals use a wide range of communication techniques. Male fiddler crabs have one claw much larger than the other to attract mates and deter rival males. Monkeys and apes use grooming to bond with each other.

DESIGN FEATURES

- Voice modules include speech and singing
- "Organ pipe" amplification of sounds by throat and nose
- Available languages include Chinese, English, Spanish, and hundreds of others.
- Language enables information to be transmitted between generations
- Widest range of facial expression in the animal kingdom.

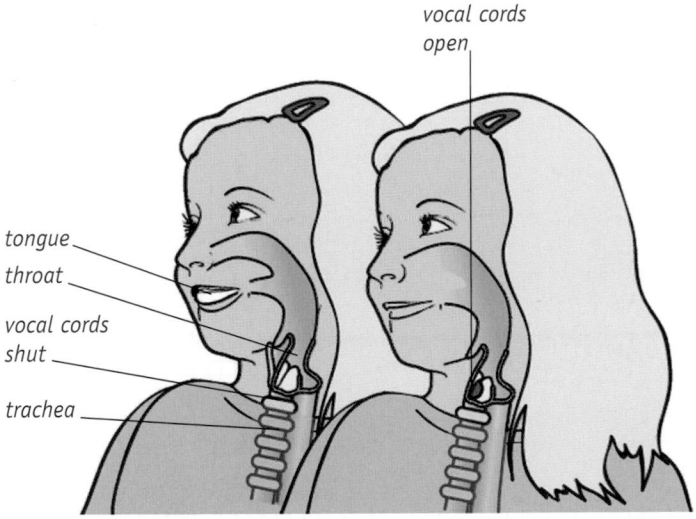

SPEECH

The larynx sits on the trachea, the tube that leads to the lungs. Stretched across the larynx are two vocal cords. During normal breathing these are wide open. When we speak they are stretched shut. Controlled bursts of air from the lungs make the stretched vocal cords vibrate and produce sounds. These sounds are turned into understandable speech by the tongue, teeth, and lips.

ADDITIONAL DATA

Sign language is used by many people who find hearing difficult. Finger, hand, arm, and body movements, along with facial expressions and lip patterns, are used as a substitute for speech.

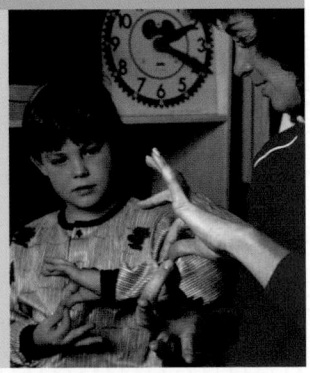

SPOT CHECK

Q. Which side of the brain controls speech?

a) Both sides b) Left c) Right.

WEB LINK KEYWORD **COMMUNICATION**

Answers: True or False? – False; Spot Check – b)

HEATING AND COOLING

Regardless of whether the outside world is boiling hot or freezing cold the temperature inside the body machine must be kept constant. Why? Because otherwise its trillions of cells refuse to work at their best. Body heat is generated mainly by the busy liver and moving muscles, spread by the blood, and then lost through the skin.

RIVAL PRODUCTS

The body temperature of reptiles, such as this lizard, changes with the outside temperature. On cool mornings, lizards bask in the sun to warm themselves so they become active. In hot, tropical countries, termites build tall nests with built-in "air-conditioning" to keep the insect colony cool during the day and warm during the chilly night.

TOO HOT

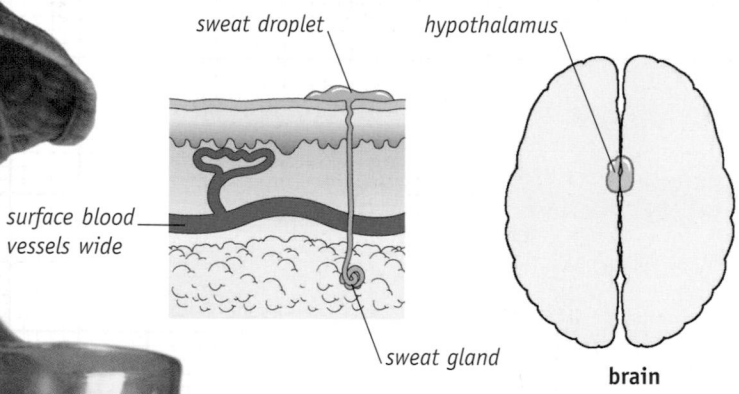

DESIGN FEATURES

- Body temperature thermostat in brain
- Various clothing options for hot and cold conditions
- Large skin surface to lose heat in hot conditions
- Optional shivering and goose bumps in cold conditions
- Automatic cooling sweat dispensers in skin.

STAYING THE SAME

To cope with changing outside temperatures, the brain's hypothalamus controls heat loss through the skin. When it's very hot, blood vessels in the skin get wider and lose extra heat from the warm blood they are carrying. The skin's sweat glands release sweat, which evaporates from the skin's surface to cool the body down. When it's cold, blood vessels get narrower so less heat is lost.

TEST YOUR PRODUCT

SWEAT TEST

Put your hand inside a clear plastic bag. Use an elastic band to loosely hold the bag around your wrist. Look at the bag over the next 30 minutes. You should be able to see tiny water droplets that have evaporated from sweat on your skin.

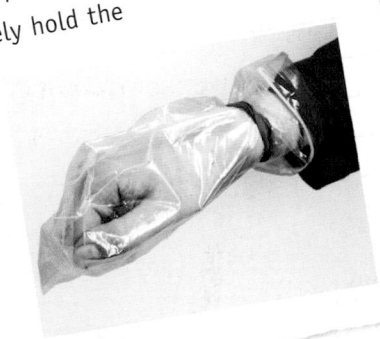

TOO COLD

? TRUE OR FALSE?

You lose over 30 percent of body heat through your head

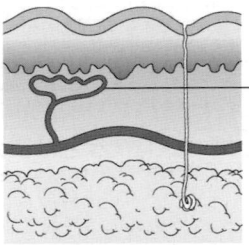

SPOT CHECK

Q. What is normal body temperature for humans?

a) 116.6°F

b) 98.6°F

c) 80.6°F.

WEB LINK KEYWORD **HEAT**

Answers: True or false? – True; Spot Check – b)

CHEMICAL CONTROL

The nervous system isn't the sole body controller. The endocrine system consists of several glands that release chemical messengers called hormones into the bloodstream. Each hormone changes the activity of specific targets. Feedback mechanisms, which work a bit like a room thermostat, maintain the right levels of each hormone in the blood.

? TRUE OR FALSE?

Hormones take much longer to work than the nervous system

EMPTY

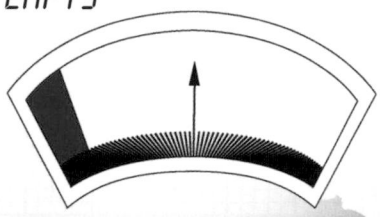

FULL

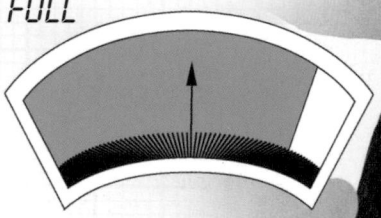

GLUCOSE LEVELS

It's vital to keep constant levels of glucose fuel in the blood regardless of whether the human machine is empty (between meals) or full (after a meal). Two hormones, called insulin and glucagon, ensure that cells are neither deprived of, nor swamped with, glucose.

MASTER GLAND

Hanging from the base of the brain, the small pituitary gland is vitally important. Overseen by the brain's hypothalamus, the pituitary releases hormones that control growth and other body functions. It also triggers other endocrine glands to release hormones that control metabolism, the rate at which the body processes and uses nutrients.

DESIGN FEATURES

- Efficient transport of hormones in bloodstream
- Network of endocrine glands in head, neck, and trunk
- Feedback system automatically regulates hormone levels
- Designated target tissues
- Long-term effects.

HORMONES IN ACTION

Hormones control a very wide range of activities. Adrenal gland hormones help us manage stress (right).

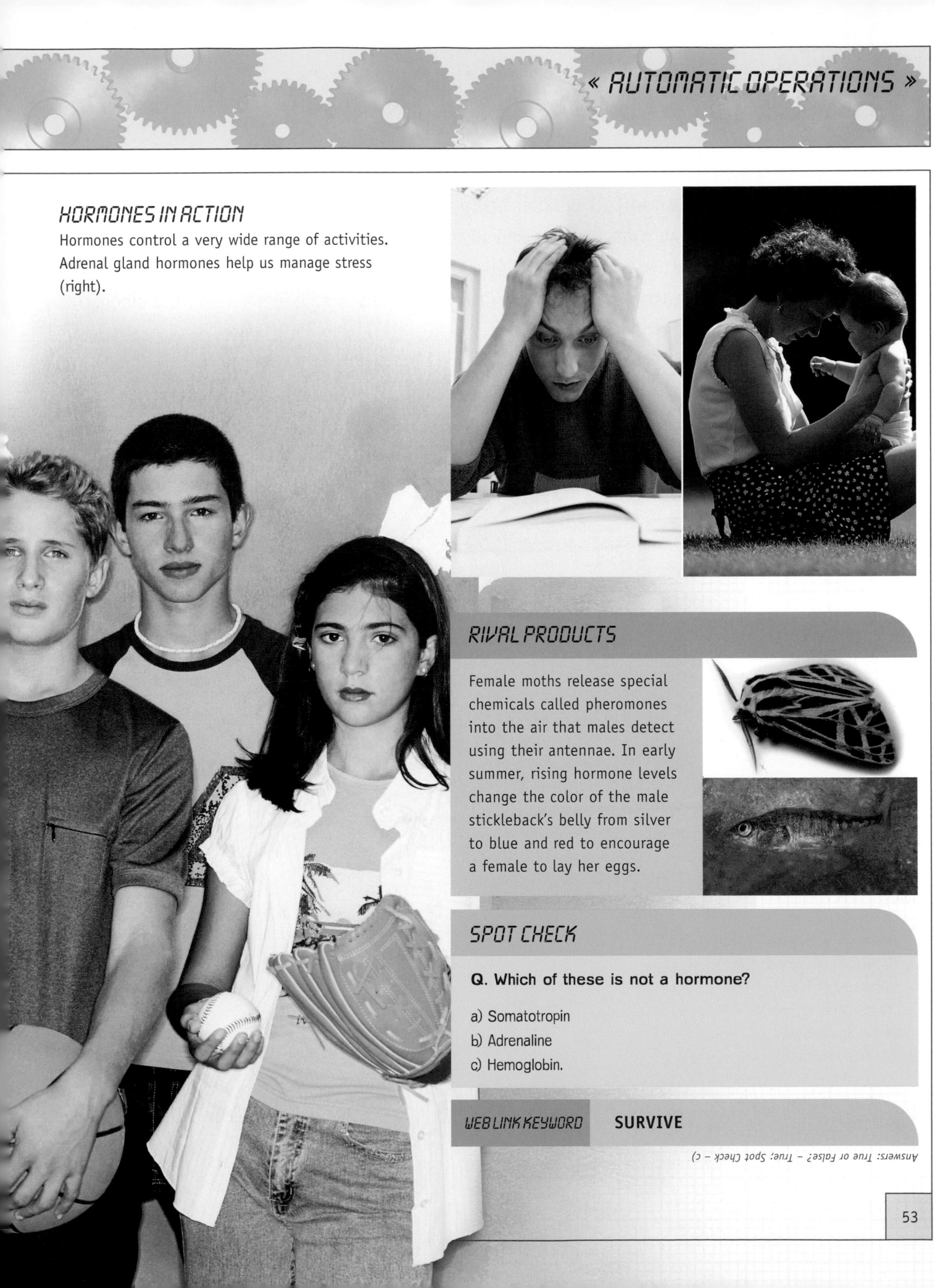

RIVAL PRODUCTS

Female moths release special chemicals called pheromones into the air that males detect using their antennae. In early summer, rising hormone levels change the color of the male stickleback's belly from silver to blue and red to encourage a female to lay her eggs.

SPOT CHECK

Q. Which of these is not a hormone?

a) Somatotropin
b) Adrenaline
c) Hemoglobin.

WEB LINK KEYWORD **SURVIVE**

Answers: True or false? – True; Spot Check – c)

WASTE AND WATER

The kidneys filter unwanted wastes made by cells from the blood, along with excess water. Inside the kidneys millions of microscopic tubes called nephrons filter fluid from the blood. Most of the water and dissolved substances are returned to the bloodstream, leaving waste and water, which are released from the body as urine.

BLOOD FILTER

Every day 3,805 pints of blood flow through the kidneys. Fluid that could fill almost 423 pint bottles is filtered from blood into the nephrons. But just 3.2 pints of waste and water pass out as urine.

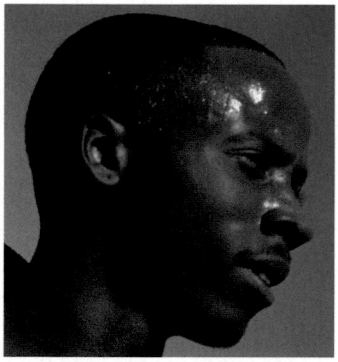

HOT SWEAT

Some water and a little waste is also lost from the body as sweat, especially on hot days, or during exercise. The more water that is lost by sweating, the lower the volume of urine produced by the kidneys.

ADDITIONAL DATA

Water is essential for life, which is why keeping constant levels of water inside the body is so important. Water content varies with age and sex. For example infants are 73% water, young men 60%, young women 50%, and older persons 45%.

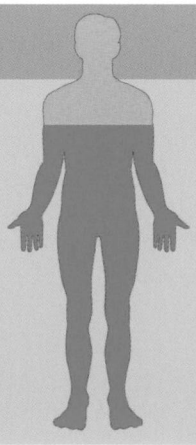

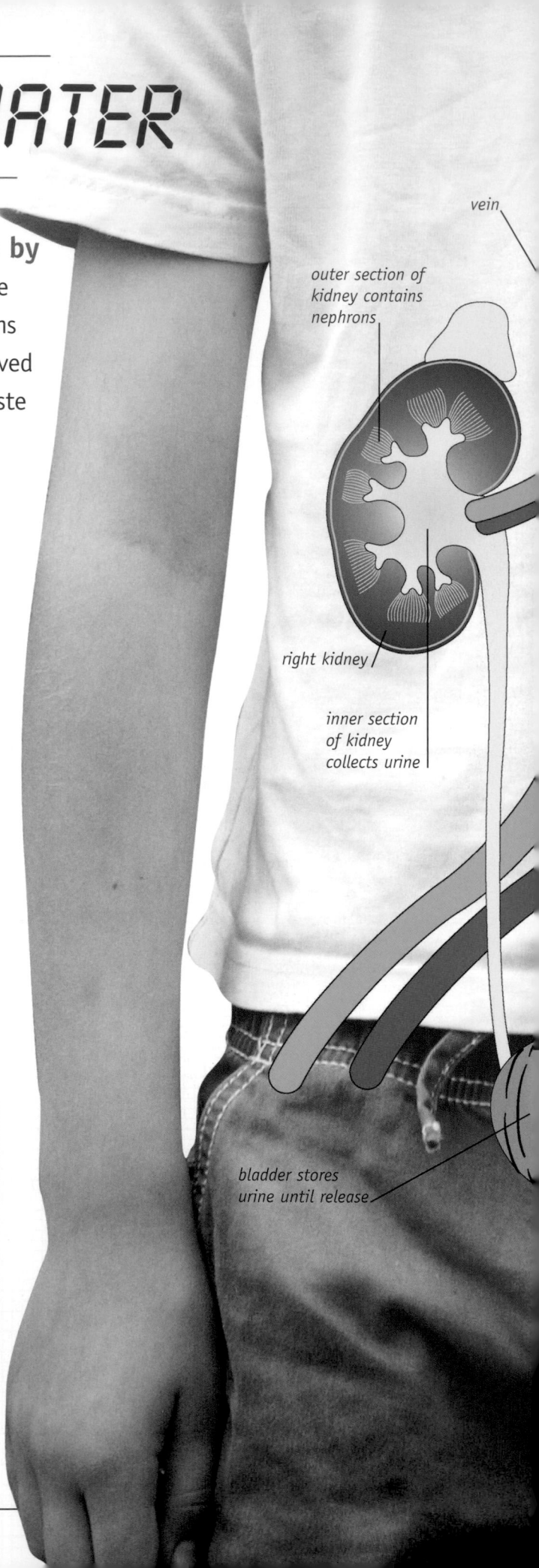

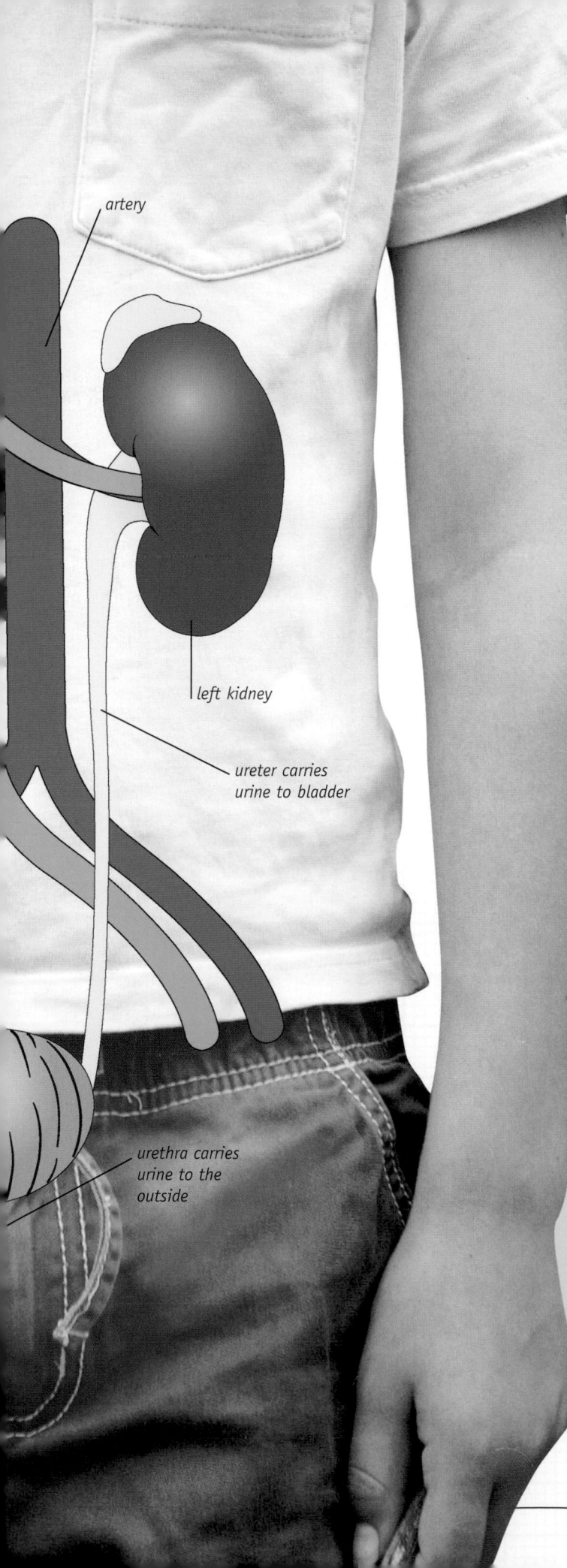

DESIGN FEATURES

- Built-in sensor in brain warns of low water levels in body by producing sensation of thirst
- Kidneys filter blood and produce urine every second of the day
- Urine released several times a day when convenient
- Warning system tells brain when bladder is full.

? TRUE OR FALSE?

Doctors can diagnose diseases by measuring levels of substances in urine

RIVAL PRODUCTS

If the kidneys stop working properly, a dialysis machine, or artificial kidney, can be used to remove waste products and excess water from the blood. The process usually takes up to six hours and is performed several times a week.

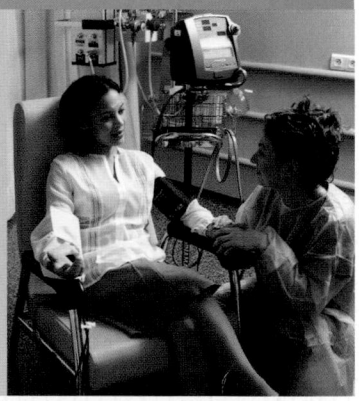

SPOT CHECK

Q. Which is the main waste substance in urine?

a) Uric acid
b) Carbon dioxide
c) Urea.

WEB LINK KEYWORD **WASTE**

Answers: True or false? – True; Spot Check – c)

SURVIVAL MODE

Humans live on most parts of the Earth and have learned to deal with extremes of cold, heat, and altitude. Survival strategies include wearing clothes to keep warm, building shelters and homes, and exploiting new sources of food.

COLD NORTH

The Inuit peoples of Greenland, northern Canada, Alaska, and Siberia are experts in surviving in some of the coldest, harshest conditions on Earth. The fish, seals, whales, musk oxen, and other polar animals that they hunt traditionally provide food, heat, light, tools, and shelter. Animal furs are made into clothes that keep out the cold. Their short, broad stature also means that they lose heat more slowly than tall, thin people.

? TRUE OR FALSE?

On mountaintops there is more oxygen in the air than at sea level

ADDITIONAL DATA

Below 80.6°F the naked body machine is no longer able to keep its body temperature at a steady 98.6°F without stoking up its internal "furnace" to release more heat. Wearing clothes and heating our homes helps us to stay at the optimum body temperature.

DESIGN FEATURES

- Built-in heat generation facility
- Insulating fat layer under the skin
- Inventive brain develops modern technology to aid survival
- Intelligent brain enables body machine to develop strategies to adapt to extremes of climate
- Heat loss system (sweating) to survive hot conditions.

LOW OXYGEN

In conditions of low or no oxygen, the human machine cannot operate. But technology allows us to get around this problem. In space, where there is no oxygen, an air supply and pressurized suit keep astronauts alive. Underwater, where the small amount of oxygen can't be breathed, a scuba diver carries an air supply.

RIVAL PRODUCTS

To survive cold winters, the dormouse surrounds itself with leaves and grasses and goes into a state of body shutdown called hibernation. In Antarctica, the coldest place on Earth, Emperor penguins huddle together to keep warm and survive the winter months.

SPOT CHECK

Q. Where is the hottest place on Earth?

a) Death Valley, California
b) Dallol Depression, Ethiopia
c) El Alizia, Libya.

WEB LINK KEYWORD **SURVIVE**

Answers: True or False? – False; Spot Check – c)

MAINTENANCE AND UPGRADES

Like any machine, the body's workings can be upset by outside interference or inner wear and tear. Internal maintenance mechanisms work to minimize damage, while upgrades may improve the way we work.

BUILT-IN PROTECTION

Normally the body machine operates without problems. But sometimes one or more parts go wrong, and we get ill. Many problems, or diseases, are caused by tiny microorganisms called pathogens or germs, including bacteria, viruses, and protists. They threaten the body 24/7, and once inside can multiply and cause disease. Fortunately, the body's defenses—the immune system—usually stop that from happening.

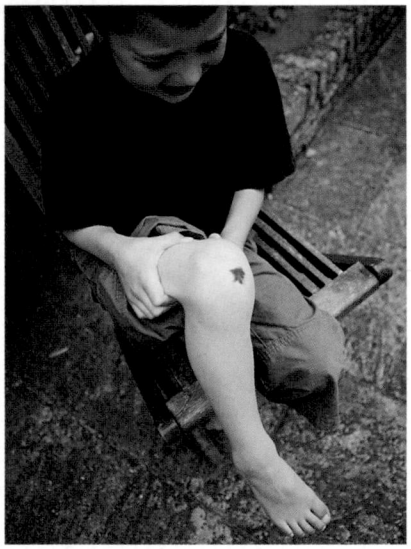

Wound healing

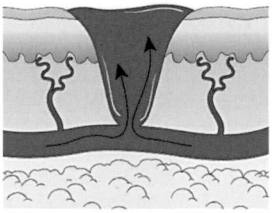

1. Cut in skin

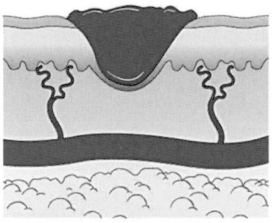

2. Clot

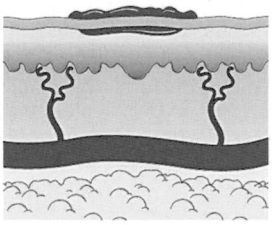

3. Scab

DEFENSES IN ACTION

If the skin, the first line of defense, gets cut (1), blood leaks out, and germs get in. Blood thickens and forms a clot (2) that dries into a scab (3), which covers the repair zone. Invading pathogens are hunted and eaten by marauding white blood cells, such as macrophages (right). If there are any escapees, chemicals called antibodies are released. These disable specific pathogens, and remember their identity should they ever invade again.

? TRUE OR FALSE?

There are over 100 different viruses that can cause the common cold

OVERREACTING

Allergies happen when the body machine's defenses overreact to something that poses no threat to it, making its owner ill. People can become sensitive to a whole range of items—called allergens—including pet hair, pollen, or foods such as peanuts.

DESIGN FEATURES

- Multilevel defenses
- First level defenses include skin, tears, saliva
- Built-in blood-clotting and scab-formation facility
- Tears and saliva contain bacteria-killing chemicals.

macrophage

bacteria

ADDITIONAL DATA

Bacteria are not the only pathogens. The flu virus (right) is one of several tiny chemical packages that cause disease in humans. Protists are one-celled organisms, some of which are pathogens, including *Giardia* (below, right), which causes really bad diarrhea.

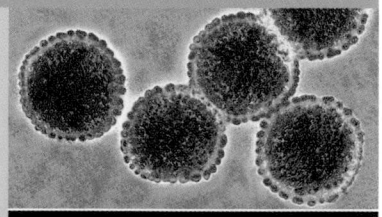

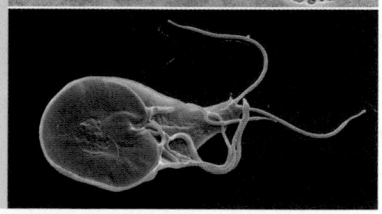

SPOT CHECK

Q. Which of these diseases is not caused by a pathogen?

a) Measles
b) Malnutrition
c) Mumps.

WEB LINK KEYWORD **PROTECT**

Answers: True or false? – True; Spot Check – b)

EMERGENCY MODE

Dangers or threats to the human machine can sometimes happen so quickly that there is no time to even think about the action you should take to avoid injury. Fortunately, the body has an emergency mode that launches automatic, high-speed reactions called reflexes that deal with danger before you are even aware of it.

TEST YOUR PRODUCT

STARTLE REFLEX

Surprise your friend. Clap your hands suddenly and loudly just in front of their face but take special care not to hit them. Their eyelids close automatically. This is an example of a reflex, in this case, one that protects the eyes from possible harm.

READY FOR ACTION

When faced with a threat, the body primes itself for action. Nerve signals from the brain, reinforced by the hormone adrenaline, cause heart and breathing rates to increase, blood glucose levels to rise, and extra blood to be diverted to muscles. These changes power up the body to run away from the threat or to confront it.

RIVAL PRODUCTS

Lizards have a neat way of getting out of trouble. If their tail is grabbed by a predator it drops off, allowing the lizard to make its escape. Some animals, such as this inflated puffer-fish, make themselves as big as possible to scare away enemies.

ADDITIONAL DATA

If you touch something sharp or hot, you pull away your hand automatically. This automatic action is called a withdrawal reflex. Nerve signals from your hand go to your spinal cord and straight back to arm muscles that pull your hand away.

DESIGN FEATURES

- Built-in body protection mechanisms
- High-speed nerve signals cause instantaneous reactions
- Adrenaline backup option available in serious situations
- Automatic reflex responses to threats.

EXTERNAL CHANGES

In a fight-or-flight situation, there are also changes that can be seen from the outside. Hair on your head stands on end to make you appear bigger. The finer hair on the rest of your body reacts in the same way, creating goose bumps. Skin goes pale, as blood is diverted, and develops a cold sweat. And in order to see more clearly, your pupils get wider to let in more light.

? TRUE OR FALSE?

Turning your head when startled is a reflex action

SPOT CHECK

How long does reflex hand withdrawal take?

a) 1 second b) 1/10 second c) 1/100 second.

WEB LINK KEYWORD **EMERGENCY**

Answers: True or false? – True; Spot Check – c)

TECHNICAL SUPPORT

They may be sophisticated and efficient, but sometimes the body's defense and repair systems need a helping hand. Accidents and disease-causing organisms, or pathogens, can threaten the body's normal workings. Fortunately, modern medicine can provide technical support in the form of diagnosis, surgery, drugs, vaccines, and other solutions to get the human machine back on track.

DESIGN FEATURES

- Wide range of treatments
- Vaccination program protects children
- Fully trained technical support specialists—doctors, dentists, nurses
- Alternative therapies available
- Body scanners image living body tissues.

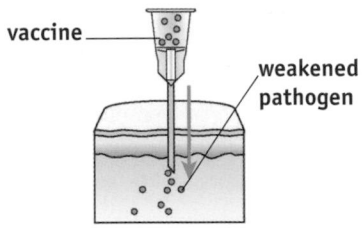

SURGERY

Surgery, the repair or replacement of diseased or damaged body tissues, takes place in the operating room. Doctors and nurses wear gowns, masks, and gloves, and use sterile instruments, to avoid infecting the patient.

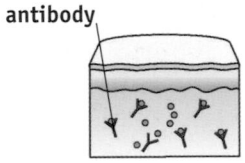

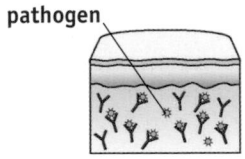

VACCINATION

Vaccination prepares the body to fight off pathogens, which can infect the body very quickly. Weakened pathogens are injected through the skin and force the defense system to make pathogen-disabling antibodies. When the "real" pathogen invades, masses of antibodies are released and infection is halted.

RIVAL PRODUCTS

Some people treat disease with "alternative" medicine. Reflexology, for example, uses foot massage to "benefit" other parts of the body. Inserting sterile needles during acupuncture "balances energy."

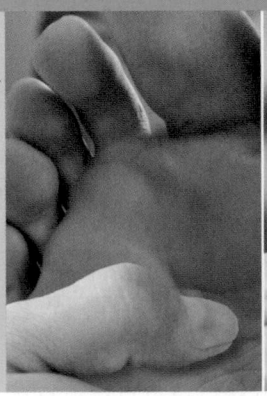

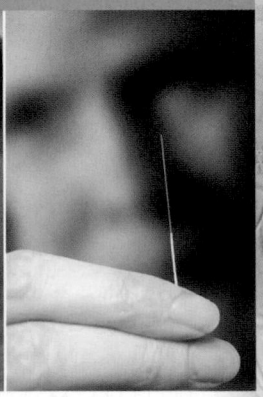

LOOKING INSIDE

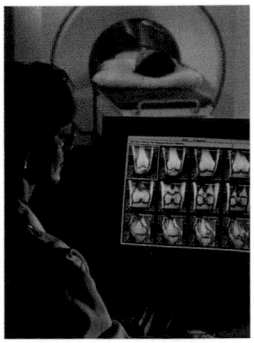

This surgeon (left) is performing "keyhole surgery" on a patient's knee. A viewing tube called an endoscope produces a picture showing the inside of the knee joint. Fine instruments passed through other incisions can be used to repair damage to the joint.

LIVING IMAGES

This CT scanner (above right) combines X rays and a computer to produce detailed images of the inside of a patient. It enables doctors to look for disease without having to cut open the body.

? TRUE OR FALSE?

Microsurgery allows severed fingers to be reattached to the hand

ADDITIONAL DATA

A doctor finds out what is wrong with a patient through diagnosis. The doctor asks questions that help establish the patient's symptoms. Careful study of these and signs of disease help the doctor identify the illness. Now treatment can be started.

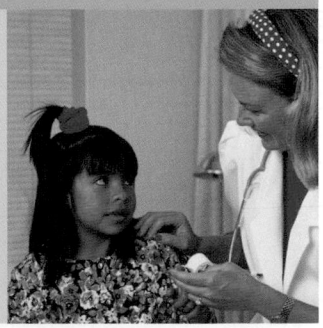

SPOT CHECK

Q. When was the first vaccination carried out?

a) 1796 b) 1896 c) 1996.

WEB LINK KEYWORD **SUPPORT**

Answers: True or false? – True; Spot Check – a)

TROUBLESHOOTING TIPS

The best way to keep the human machine working smoothly and in tip-top condition is to take good care of it. Regular exercise—preferably every day—is important for fitness. It also helps to keep the body's weight at the right level, in combination with eating a balanced diet.

IMPROVED SPECIFICATION

All parts of the body benefit if you keep fit. The brain will work faster and allow you to think more clearly. The heart and lungs will run more efficiently. Bones will be stronger, while muscles will have more pulling power and tire less easily.

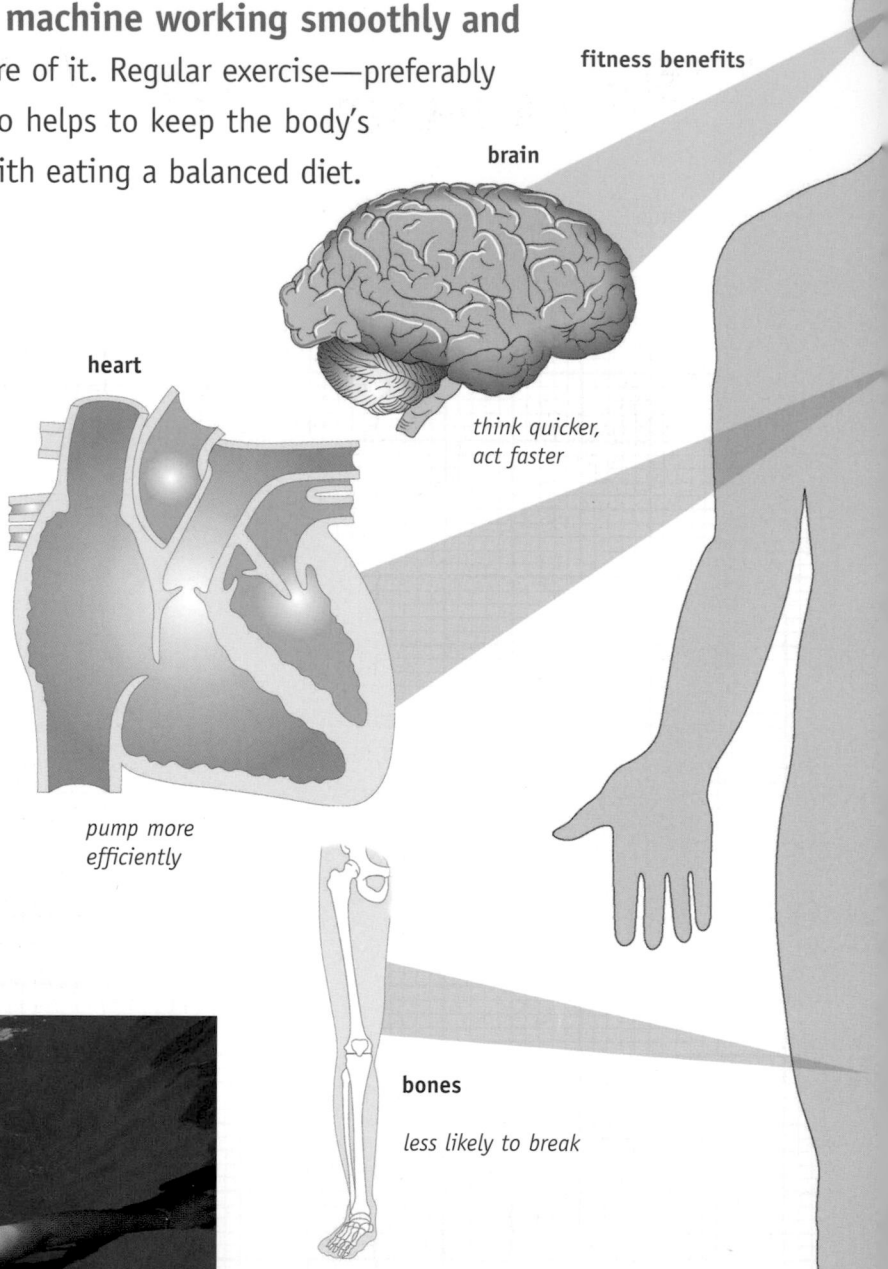

EXERCISE

To stay fit, you need to exercise daily. Regular walking or running increases your stamina—how efficiently your heart, lungs, and muscles work. Other activities, such as cycling, increase muscle strength. Dance and yoga are good for keeping the body flexible. And swimming increases all three—stamina, strength, and flexibility.

? TRUE OR FALSE? Milk contains calcium needed for bone and tooth growth

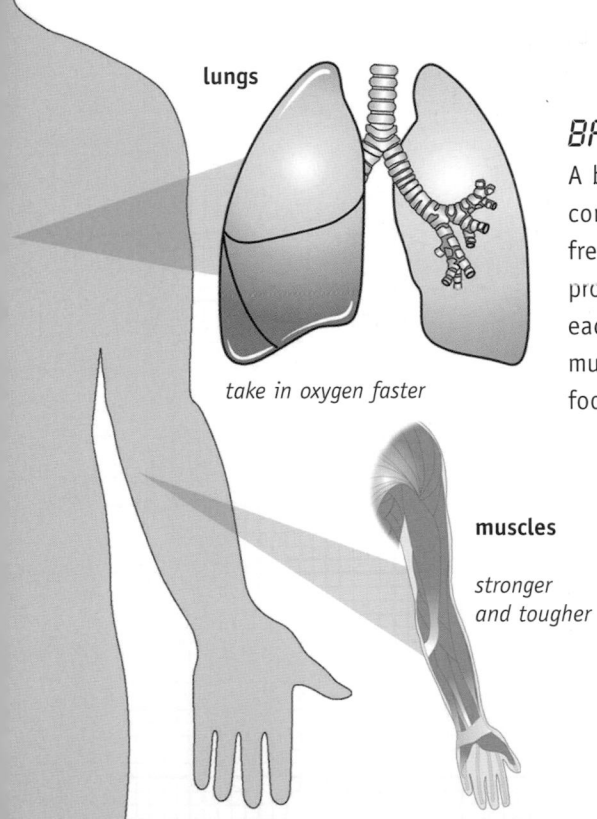

BALANCED DIET

A balanced diet is one that contains a wide range of different fresh foods. The food pyramid provides a guide. The size of each segment shows how much of each type of food the body needs.

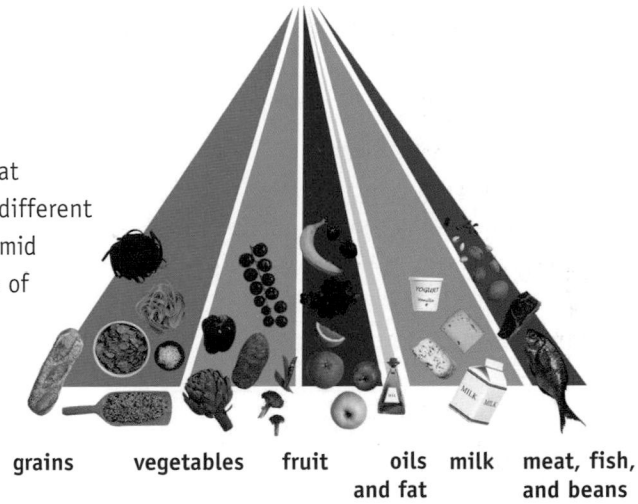

RIVAL PRODUCTS

Clay is an important part of the tapir's diet. It is believed that clay particles in the stomach remove poisons found in the plants this animal eats. On chilly mornings, bumblebees need to warm up by "shivering" before they are able to take off and fly.

ADDITIONAL DATA

A diet of junk food, combined with a lack of exercise, can lead to serious problems, such as obesity, heart disease, and diabetes. Junk foods are usually rich in fat, sugar, and salt, but lack vitamins and fiber.

SPOT CHECK

Q. Which food is rich in protein, the nutrient needed for body growth and repair?

a) Tomatoes b) Tuna c) Pasta.

WEB LINK KEYWORD **TROUBLESHOOTING**

Answers: True or False? – True; Spot Check – b)

MECHANICAL FAILURE

Despite having built-in defenses and technical support, the body, like any machine, is at risk of mechanical breakdown. General wear and tear or lack of care can result in serious life-threatening problems. These include heart attacks, strokes, and some cancers.

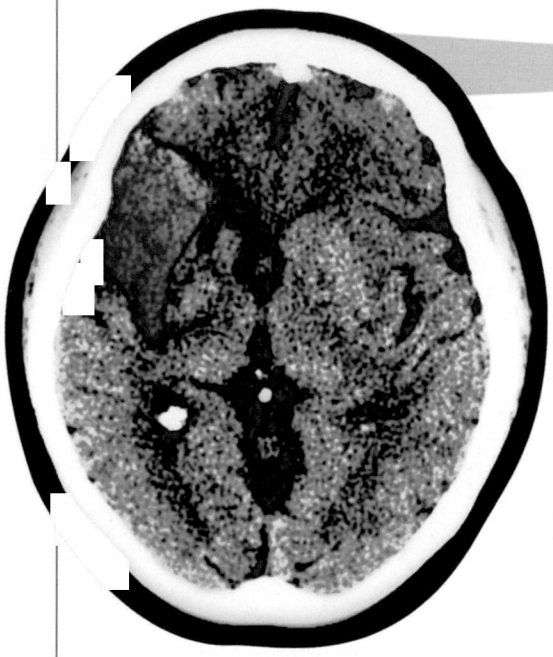

STROKE

When the blood supply to part of the brain is cut off, the result is a stroke, as shown by this red patch on a CT scan of the brain (green). A stroke may be caused by arteries that become blocked or burst. Without oxygen the affected area of the brain stops working properly.

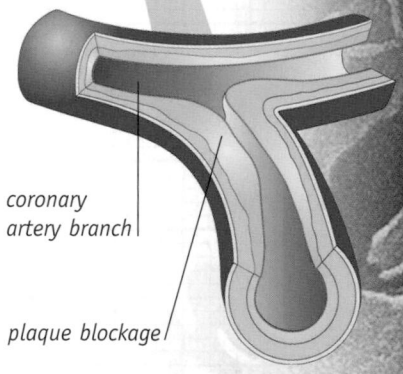

HEART DISEASE

The coronary artery supplies the beating heart muscle with blood. If there is a build-up of fatty plaque, this can halt the blood supply. In turn, this can lead to a heart attack and stop the heart from beating.

RIVAL PRODUCTS

We are not alone when it comes to mechanical failure. Other animals have heart problems, strokes, and cancers, and are treated by veterinarians. Even plants don't escape major breakdowns. A disease called bleeding canker can destroy the bark of trees, such as this horse chestnut.

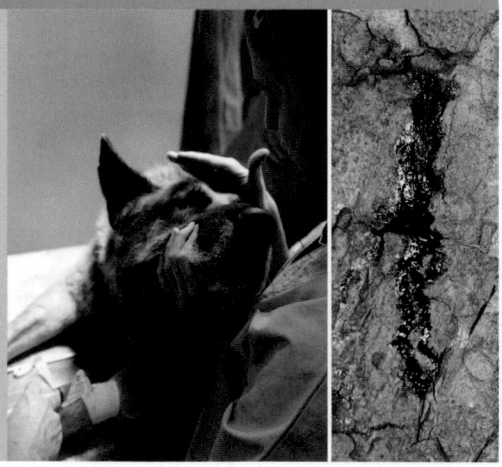

? TRUE OR FALSE?

Mechanical failure is more likely to happen in older people

DESIGN FEATURES

- Abnormal cell division can cause cancers
- Blocked or broken blood vessels can upset brain activity
- Blocked blood vessels can stop the heart from working properly
- Lifestyle factors, such as diet and exercise, can increase the risk of mechanical failure.

CANCERS

This cancer cell (pink) is out of control. Cancer cells are abnormal body cells. They divide uncontrollably to form tumors (lumps) that spread into and stop parts of the body, such as the lungs, from working properly. Fortunately, defense cells (blue) usually kill cancer cells before they can multiply and cause harm.

ADDITIONAL DATA

To prevent a heart attack, or to help after one, a medical procedure called angioplasty opens up a blockage in one of the heart's coronary arteries. A small balloon is inflated to widen the blood vessel. A device called a stent is then left behind to keep the vessel open.

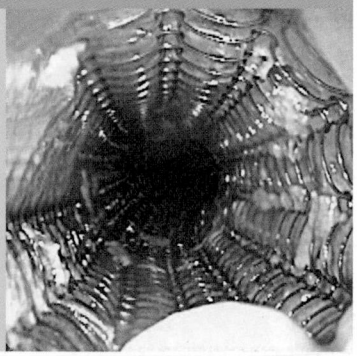

SPOT CHECK

Q. What is the best way to avoid mechanical failure?

a) Eating junk foods
b) Exercising every day
c) Watching TV.

WEB LINK KEYWORD **FAILURE**

Answers: True or False? – True; Spot Check – b)

PARTS AND UPGRADES

Modern medicine is able to supply the human machine with an increasing range of spare parts to replace components that have been damaged, worn out, or lost. These include artificial arms with motorized fingers, replacement joints, or new lenses for the eyes. In addition, transplantation means that major organs, such as the heart or kidneys, can be transferred, during an operation, from one human machine to another.

ORGAN TRANSPLANTS

Kidney transplants involve taking a healthy kidney from a suitable donor—either living or recently deceased—and putting it inside the body of a person with damaged kidneys. Here, the surgeon is attaching the replacement kidney, and connecting it to the blood supply.

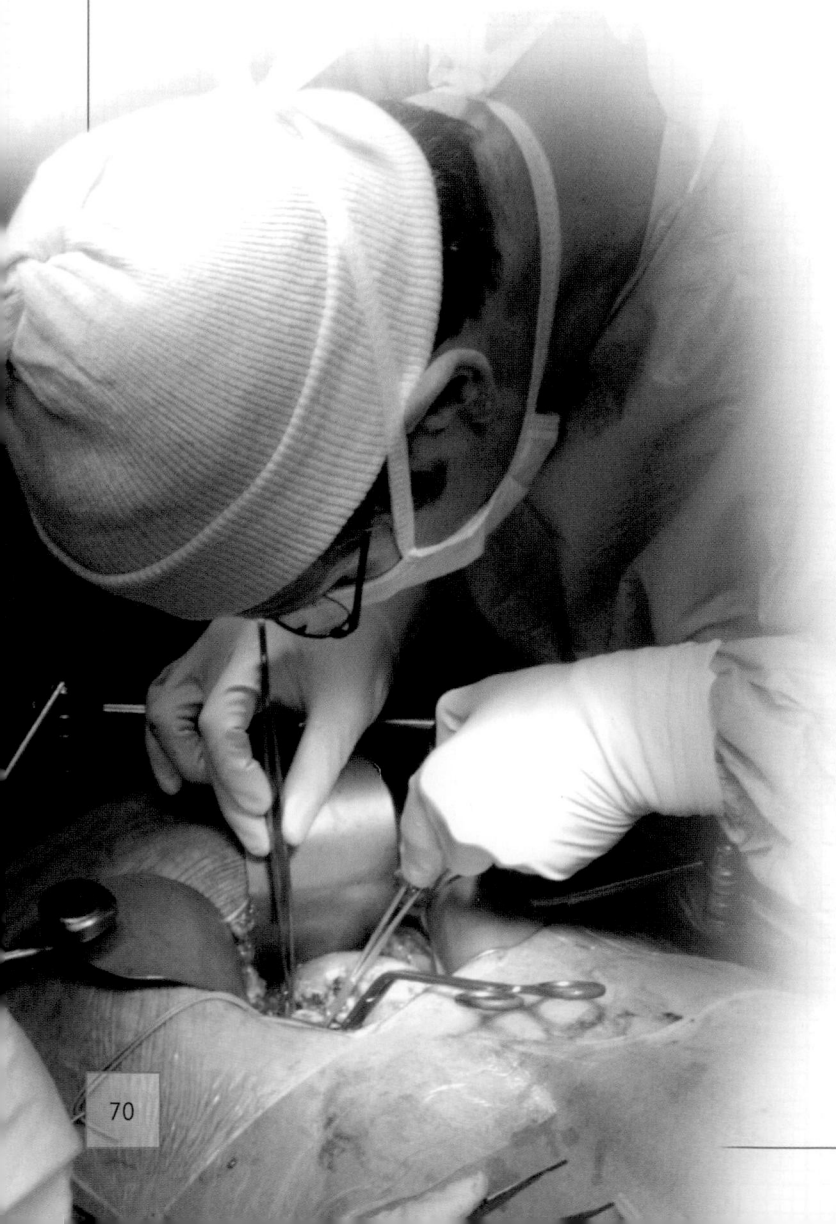

DESIGN FEATURES

- Transplants can replace a damaged heart, kidney, liver, or lung
- Custom-built spare parts made from high-grade metals and plastics
- Potential to grow replacement parts
- Possibility of future upgrades to improve body machine performance.

RIVAL PRODUCTS

If humans lose all or part of a limb we would not expect it to grow back. But this process, called regeneration, does happen in "simple" animals, such as starfish. When tree branches are cut back—a process called pollarding—new shoots grow from around the cut area.

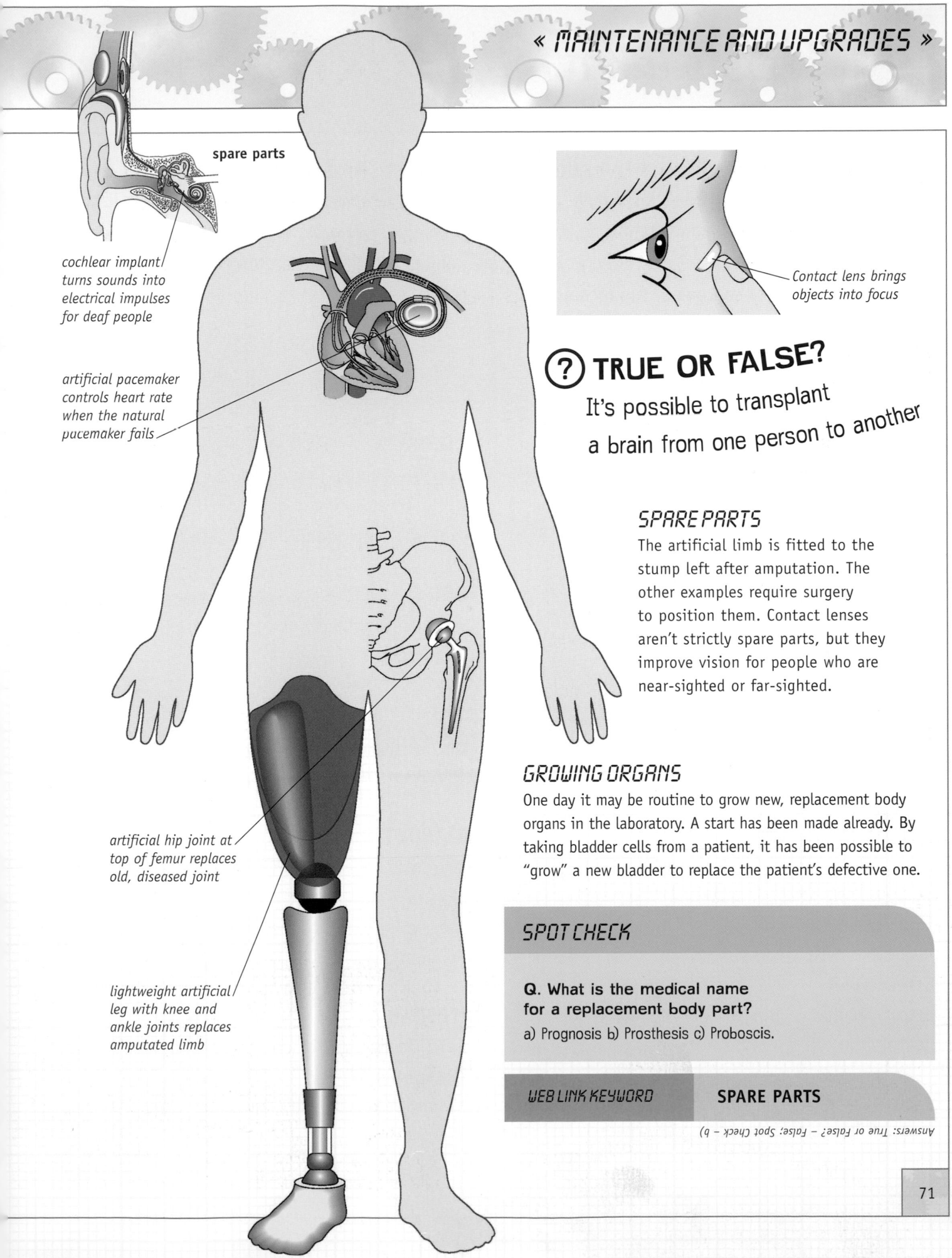

? TRUE OR FALSE?

It's possible to transplant a brain from one person to another

SPARE PARTS

The artificial limb is fitted to the stump left after amputation. The other examples require surgery to position them. Contact lenses aren't strictly spare parts, but they improve vision for people who are near-sighted or far-sighted.

GROWING ORGANS

One day it may be routine to grow new, replacement body organs in the laboratory. A start has been made already. By taking bladder cells from a patient, it has been possible to "grow" a new bladder to replace the patient's defective one.

SPOT CHECK

Q. What is the medical name for a replacement body part?

a) Prognosis b) Prosthesis c) Proboscis.

WEB LINK KEYWORD **SPARE PARTS**

Answers: True or False? – False; Spot Check – b)

WEBLINKS

Look at the bottom of each right-hand page in the book and you will find a WEBLINK. For each WEBLINK we have recommended websites that provide additional fascinating information about the human machine in the form of animations, quizzes, and articles. Please note that the content of a website may change at any time, and that neither the publisher nor the author is responsible for any content of the recommended websites. Ask an adult to help you find additional websites and check them out before you use them.

BIOMECHANICS

www.bbc.co.uk/science/humanbody/body/interactives/3djigsaw_02/index.shtml?skeleton
http://insideout.rigb.org/ri/anatomy/casing_the_joint/joints_explorer.html

CELLS

www.icnet.uk/kids/cellsrus/cellsrus.html
www.cellsalive.com/

CIRCULATION

http://www.blood.co.uk/pages/bbits.htm

COMMUNICATION

www.phon.ox.ac.uk/~jcoleman/phonation.htm
www.pbs.org/wnet/soundandfury/culture/sign_flash5.html

COMPUTER

http://faculty.washington.edu/chudler/neurok.htm

FAILURE

http://media.med.cornell.edu/swf/bal_ang.html
http://www.mercymed.com/vascular/discoveries/images/balloon_stent/balloon_stent.mov

FUEL

www.medicalanimations.com/video.php?num=35&type=mov

HEAT

http://www.abpischools.org.uk/resources/skin/skin3.asp

INSTRUCTIONS

http://gslc.genetics.utah.edu/units/basics/tour/
http://ology.amnh.org/genetics/youYou/youyou.html

LIFESPAN

http://kidshealth.org/kid/grow/body_stuff/puberty.html
www.omsi.edu/visit/life/aging/intro.cfm

MEMORY
www.bbc.co.uk/science/humanbody/mind surveys/memory
http://faculty.washington.edu/chudler/java/facemem.html

PROTECT
http://medmyst.rice.edu/html/mission1.htm

SKIN
http://magma.nationalgeographic.com/ngexplorer/0206/quickflicks/

SLEEP
http://www.brainpop.com/health/nervoussystem/sleep/

SPARE PARTS
www.kidneypatientguide.org.uk/site/TRAanim.php
www.pbs.org/wgbh/nova/eheart/manmade.html

SPECIFICATION
http://kidshealth.org/PageManager.jsp?lic=1&article_set=29673&ps=110
www.medtropolis.com/VBody.asp

SUPPORT
www.edheads.org/activities/knee/
www.pbs.org/wgbh/aso/tryit/doctor/

SURVIVE
http://www.kativik.net/ulluriaq/Nunavik/inuitlife/index.html

TESTS
www.michaelbach.de/ot/
http://lite.bu.edu/vision/applets/lite/lite/lite.html

TROUBLESHOOTING
http://www.coolfoodplanet.org/gb/kidz/
www.lifebytes.gov.uk/eating/eat_menu.html

VENTILATION
www.bmu.unimelb.edu.au/examples/gasxlung/

VISION
http://insideout.rigb.org/ri/anatomy/tissue_issues/eye_eye.html

WASTE
http://www.kidshealth.org/kid/body/kidneys_sw.html

WIRING http://getyourwebsitehere.com/jswb/rttest01.html

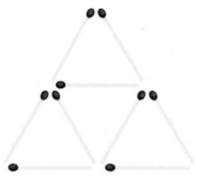

Here's the answer to the brainteaser on page 37.

GLOSSARY

ADOLESCENCE
The period during the teen years when, through a series of physical and mental changes, a child develops into an adult.

ANTIBODY
A chemical released by white blood cells of the immune system that targets a specific disease-causing germ and marks it for destruction.

ARTERY
A thick-walled blood vessel that carries blood away from the heart toward organs and tissues.

ARTHROPOD
One of a very large group of animals without backbones that have a hard outer skeleton and jointed limbs and which include insects, spiders, and crustaceans.

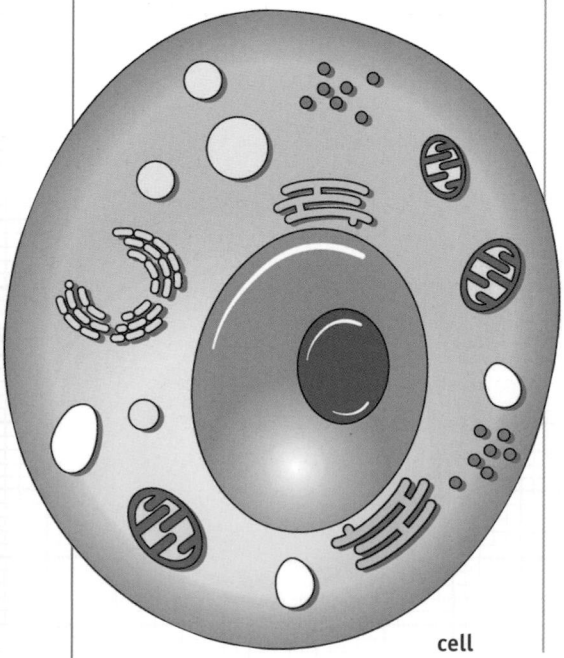

cell

ATRIUM (plural: atria)
One of the two—left and right—upper chambers of the heart.

BACTERIUM (plural: bacteria)
A single-celled organism that belongs to the most abundant group of living things on Earth, some of which cause disease in humans.

BILLION
A number equivalent to one thousand million (1,000,000,000).

CAPILLARY
A microscopic blood vessel that supplies food and oxygen to individual cells in the tissues and links the smallest arteries to the smallest veins.

CARBON DIOXIDE
A gas that is the poisonous waste product of energy release by the cells. It is breathed out into the air from the lungs.

CENTRAL NERVOUS SYSTEM (CNS)
The controlling and coordinating section of the nervous system, which consists of the brain and spinal cord. It is connected to the rest of the body by nerves.

CEREBRUM
The largest part of the brain, divided into left and right hemispheres, which control opposite sides of the body. The cerebrum is responsible for thought, emotions, sensing, and movement.

DERMIS
The thicker, inner layer of the skin found beneath the protective epidermis. It contains blood vessels, sweat glands, and sensors.

DNA (Deoxyribonucleic acid)
One of a set of large molecules found in the nucleus of every cell. DNA contains the coded instructions to build and operate that cell.

EEG (Electroencephalogram)
A recording of electrical activity in the brain (brainwaves) made by a machine called an electroencephalograph.

ENDOCRINE SYSTEM
A collection of assorted glands, including the pituitary gland, that release chemical messengers called hormones into the bloodstream.

ENZYME
A chemical that greatly speeds up the rate of chemical reactions, including those that break down food during digestion.

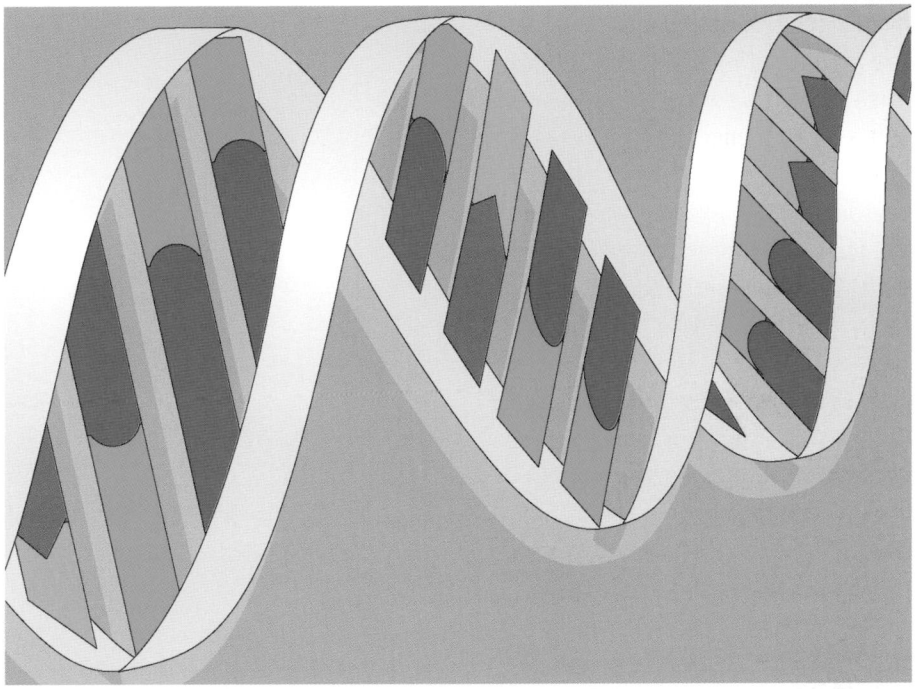

DNA

EPIDERMIS
The thinner, upper layer of the skin above the dermis. The cells of the epidermis are constantly worn away and replaced.

ER (Endoplasmic reticulum)
A network of folded membranes inside a cell that makes, stores, and transports substances.

GENE
One of around 25,000 instructions for making and running a human body stored in the DNA molecules inside cells.

GOLGI BODY
A series of flattened membrane "bags" found inside cells that package and transport newly made substances.

GLUCOSE
A sugar obtained from food during digestion that circulates in the blood and provides the body's main source of energy.

HYPOTHALAMUS
A part of the brain that regulates many body activities and links the nervous and endocrine systems.

IMMUNE SYSTEM
The body's defense system, which consists mainly of various types of white blood cells that protect against infection by pathogens.

GLOSSARY

INFRARED RADIATION
Rays produced by a hot object, such as the Sun, that makes us feel warm.

JOINT
The part of the skeleton where two or more bones meet and which enables movement to occur.

LARYNX
Also called the voice box, the part of the respiratory system that contains vocal cords and produces sounds.

LIVER
The body's largest internal organ, which performs over 500 functions to control the chemical content of the blood.

MITOCHONDRION
(plural: mitochondria)
One of several spherical or sausage-shaped organelles found inside cells that release the energy needed to power cell activities.

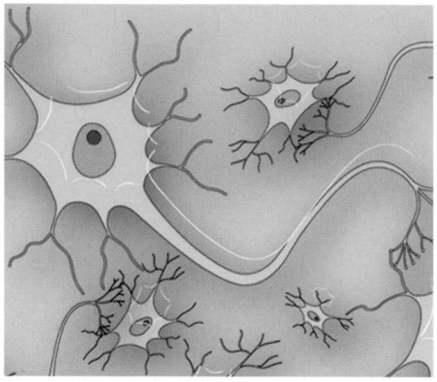
neurons

MOLECULE
A chemical unit made up of two or more linked tiny particles called atoms.

MUSCLE
A body organ or tissue that is capable of contracting (getting shorter) in order to produce movement.

NANOTECHNOLOGY
The branch of technology that involves the construction of structures at the microscopic level using atoms and molecules.

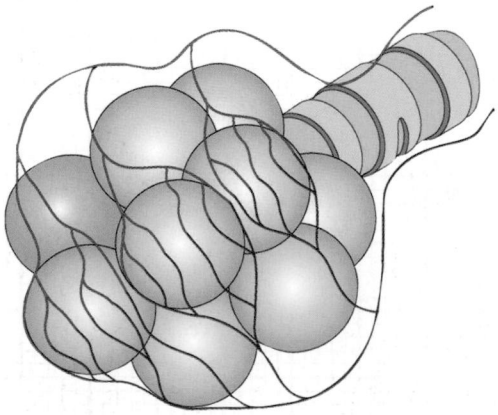
alveoli

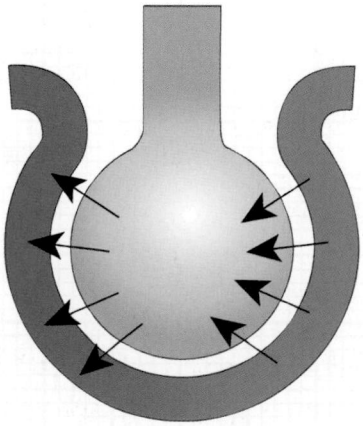
gas exchange

NEURON
One of the billions of interconnected nerve cells that make up the nervous system and can carry high-speed electrical signals called impulses.

NREM (nonrapid eye movement) SLEEP
The stages of deep sleep that recur during the night—between phases of REM sleep—and during which body activities fall to a minimum.

NUCLEUS
The control center of cell which contains DNA.

NUTRIENT
A substance that your body needs to work properly and keep you alive. Nutrients are found in food and drink.

ORGANELLE
A microscopic structure inside a cell, such as ER or a mitochondrion, that has a specific job to do.

ORGAN
A key part of the body, such as the kidney or brain, that is made up of two or more types of tissue and has one or more specific roles.

OXYGEN
A gas found in the air that is breathed in and used by cells to release energy from glucose.

PATHOGEN
A microscopic organism, such as certain types of bacteria, viruses, and protists that cause disease in humans.

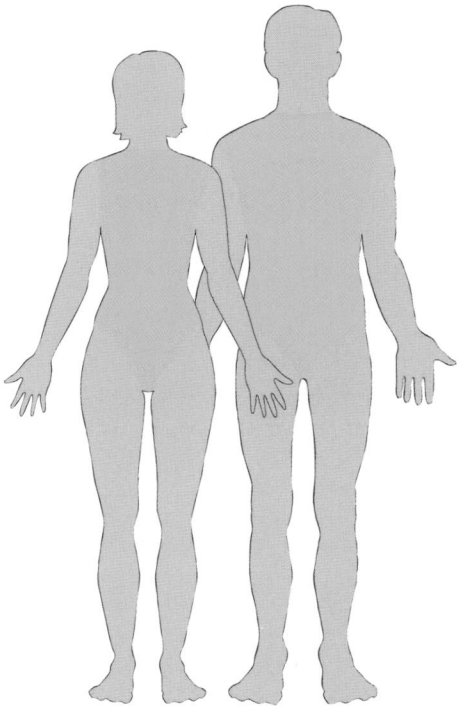

PLASMA
The liquid part of blood that is mainly water. Plasma contains many dissolved substances.

PROTIST
A member of a group of single-celled organisms—larger and more complex than bacteria—some of which cause disease in humans.

REFLEX
An automatic, split-second and unchanging response by the body that often protects it from danger.

REM (rapid eye movement) SLEEP
The stage of lighter sleep that occurs during the night—between phases of NREM (nonrapid eye movement) sleep—when the brain is active, the body apart from the eyes is paralyzed, and dreaming takes place.

SKELETAL MUSCLE
The type of muscle that is attached to the skeleton and shapes and moves the body.

TISSUE
A collection of one type, or similar types, of cell that work together to perform a particular function. Different tissues join together to form an organ.

TRILLION
A number equivalent to one million million (1,000,000,000,000).

TRUNK
The central part of the body, consisting of the chest and abdomen, to which the head and limbs are attached. It is also known as the torso.

ULTRASOUND
High-frequency sound waves that are used to produce images inside the body, including those of a developing fetus.

VEIN
A blood vessel that carries blood away from tissues and organs back toward the heart.

VENTRICLE
One of the two—left and right—lower chambers of the heart.

VIRUS
One of a group of very small, nonliving chemical packages that cause diseases such as colds, flu, and measles. Viruses infect and destroy body cells in order to reproduce.

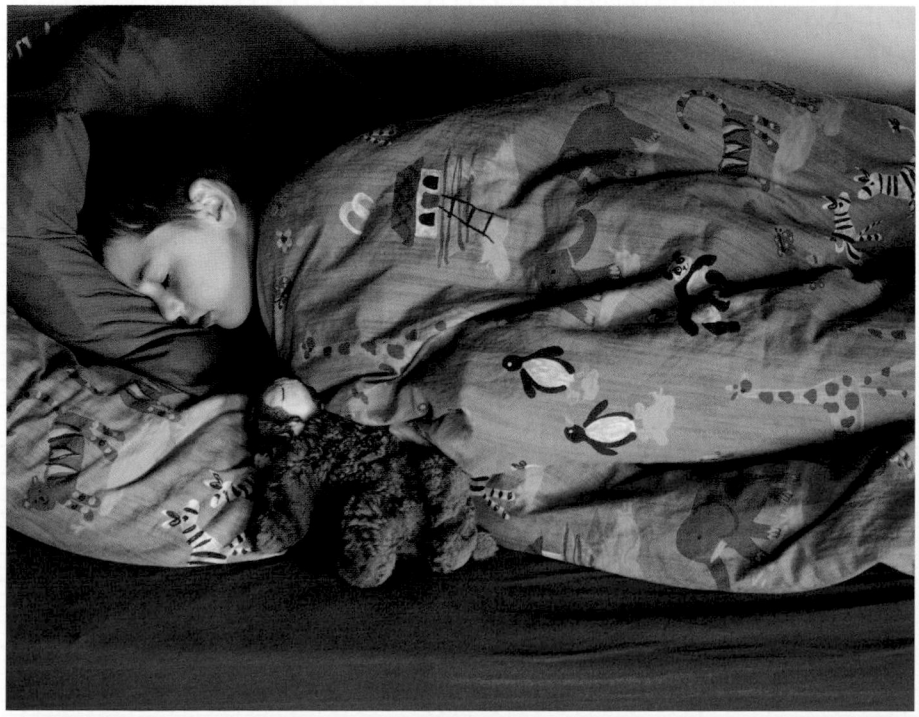

INDEX

A
acupuncture 64
adolescence 15, 74
adrenaline 62
adulthood 15
ageing 14–15
allergens 61
allergies 61
alveoli 33
angioplasty 69
antibodies 64, 74
ants 37
arteries 28, 68, 74
artificial blood 29
artificial limbs 71
atoms 17
atria 28, 74

B
backbone 24, 25
bacteria 60, 74
balance 37
biceps 24
bladder 55, 71
blood 28–29, 50, 52, 54 60, 62, 68
blood vessels 18, 26, 28, 29, 50, 51, 69
bloodstream 34, 35, 52
body language 48
body systems 8–9
body temperature 50–51, 56
bones 24–25, 66
brain 9, 14, 24, 36–37, 38–39, 40, 44, 46, 47, 49, 50, 51, 57, 66, 68
breathing 9, 32–33, 41, 62
bronchi 32, 33

C
cancer 68, 69
capillaries 28, 33, 74
carbon dioxide 32, 33, 35, 74
cells 16–17, 26, 28, 29, 32, 34, 52, 69
central nervous system 27, 74
cerebellum 36
cerebrum 36, 37, 38, 74
chest 32
chromosomes 22
circulatory system 9, 28–29
clot 60
cochlea 43, 71
communication 48–49
computers 36, 37
contact lenses 71
cornea 44, 45
coronary artery 68
CT scans 65, 68
cytoplasm 16

D
dermis 18, 75
diagnosis 64, 65
dialysis 55
diaphragm 32
diet 66, 67
digestion 34–35
digestive system 8, 34–35
diseases 60, 61
DNA 22, 23, 75
doctors 64
dolphins 40
dominant eye 44
dreams 40

E
eardrum 43
ears 42, 43
eating 34, 66, 67
EEGs 41, 75
emotions 36, 38, 39
endocrine system 52–53, 75
endoscope 65
enzymes 34, 35, 75
epidermis 18, 74
esophagus 35
exercise 15, 29, 66
eyes 23, 32, 40, 44–45, 46

F
facial expressions 48, 49
fat (food) 67
fear 38, 39
fingernails 18, 19
fitness 66
flu virus 61
food 8, 20, 32, 34, 35, 56, 66, 67
fungi 35

G
gas exchange 33
genes 12, 14, 22–23, 75
genome 22
germs 18, 60
glands 52
glucagon 52
glucose 32, 52, 62, 75
goose bumps 63

H
hair 13, 18, 63
hearing 36, 43
heart 28, 29, 66, 68
heart attacks 68
heart rate 29, 36, 41, 62
hemispheres 37
hibernation 57
hippocampus 38
hormones 29, 52–53
hypothalamus 50, 51, 52, 75

I
immune system 60–61, 75
inheritance 22–23
insects 19
insulin 52
internet 26
intestines 35
Inuit 56
iris 45

J
joints 24, 25, 65, 76

K
keyhole surgery 65
kidneys 54–55, 70

L
larynx 49, 76
learning 39
lens 44, 45
limbic system 38, 39
limbs 12
lips 49
liver 50, 76
lungs 28, 32–33, 49, 66, 67

M
mammals 13
melanin 18
memory 38–39, 40
metabolism 52
mitochondria 16, 17, 76
molecules 34, 76
moths 53
movement 24, 36
muscles 9, 24–25, 29, 48, 50, 62, 66, 76

N
nephrons 54
nerves 9, 26, 43
nervous system 9, 26–27, 52
neurons 17, 26, 27, 36, 37, 76
nonrapid eye movement (NREM) 40, 41
nucleus 16, 76
nutrients 34, 76

O
olfactory nerve 43
optic nerve 44, 45
optical illusions 46–47
organelles 16, 76
organs 9, 12, 16, 70, 76
ovaries 53
oxygen 20, 28, 29, 32, 33, 56, 57, 67, 68, 76

P
pacemaker 71
pathogens 60, 61, 64, 76
personality 36
phobias 39
pituitary gland 52, 53
plaque 68
plasma 29, 77
protists 61, 77
puberty 53
pulse 29
pupil 44, 45, 63

R
rapid eye movement (REM) 40, 41
reaction times 27
reflexes 62–63, 77
reflexology 64
retina 44
ribs 32

S
saliva 34, 61
scabs 60
sensors 19, 42–43, 44
sign language 43
skeleton 9, 24–25
skin 15, 18–19, 50, 51, 60, 63
skull 37, 44
sleep 40–41
smell 38, 42, 43
sounds 43, 49
spare parts 70–71
speech 36, 48, 49
spiders 39
spinal cord 9, 27, 36, 38, 62
stamina 66
starch 34
stomach 34, 35
stress 15, 53
strokes 68
surgery 64–65
swallowing 35
sweat 50, 54, 63
sweat glands 50, 51

T
taste 42, 43
taste buds 42, 43
teeth 34, 49
testes 53
thalamus 38
thinking 26, 36, 38, 66
thorax 12
throat 32
tissues 16, 65, 77
tongue 43, 49
touch 36, 43
trachea (windpipe) 32, 49
trees 35
tumors 69

U
urine 54, 55
UV (ultraviolet) radiation 18, 19

V
vaccines 64
veins 28, 77
ventricles 28, 77
viruses 60, 61, 77
vision 36, 43, 44–45
vocal cords 49

W
waste disposal 28, 54–55
white blood cells 29, 60
wounds 60

ACKNOWLEDGMENTS

The publishers would like to thank the following for permission to use their material.
Every care has been taken to trace copyright holders. However, if there have been unintentional omissions or failure to trace copyright holders, we apologize, and will, if informed, endeavor to make corrections in any future edition.

KEY
t = top; c = center; b = bottom; r = right; l = left

Peter Homlboe
8–9; 15c; 17l, 18bl; 19tr; 22tc; 22–23; 23tr; 22cr; 24–25; 25tr, 27bl; 29cl; 30–31; 33l; 34l; 36–37; 37cr; 38r; 39bl; 40–41; 42–43; 43bl; 44br; 45tr; 46–47 (illustrations); 48cr; 50–51; 51tr; 52c (illustration); 54cl (illustration); 54–55; 60cl; 62c; 64bl; 75tr; 77br

Getty Images
4–5 (Dr. David Phillips); 14tcl (Georges Gobet/AFP); 18–19 (Mike Powell); 56–57 (James Balog); 57cr (Bob Eisdale); 62–63 (Tom Hussey)

Oxford University Press
1–2; 10–11; 12–13; 13cr; 14c; 14b–15b; 15tc; 19cr; 22tl; 25cr, 27; 29bl; 29cr; 32bl; 32r; 34b; 35br; 38l; 39r; 40br; 42l; 45cr; 48l; 48bl; 50ct; 52–53; 53r; 54cl; 57tl; 57cr; 58–59; 61tc; 62bl; 64–65; 65tr; 65br; 66bl; 67bl; 67cr; 70cr; 74tr; 76tc

Science Photo Library
16b (K H Kjeldsen); 17r (Alfred Pasieka), 20-21 (Ian Boddy) ; 26bl (Laguna Design); 29cl (Philippe Plailly/Eurelios); 41bc (Will and Deni McIntyre); 49r (Blair Seitz); 55r (AJ Photo/Hop Americain); 60–61 (Eye of Science); 61cr (James Cavallini) 61cb (Eye of Science); 68tl (Zephyr); 68bl (Mauro Fermariello); 68br (Georgette Douwma); 68–69 (Steve Gschmiessner); 70bl (AJ Photo)

With additional thanks to Alamy (metal cog device), Samir - the scope (69l), USDA Center for Nutrition Policy and Promotion (67tr), Ventracor Limited for image of VentrAssist™ (29cr)

Models: Matilda Ashford, Tom Ashford, Manny Campion-Dye, Ruben Cleghorn, Oli Jones, Polly Rawlings, Madeline Rolt

Illustrations by Dee McLean/Linden Artists